THE DEVELOPING CHILD

Recent decades have witnessed unprecedented advances in research on human development. In those same decades there have been profound changes in public policy toward children. Each book in the Developing Child series reflects the importance of such research in its own right and as it bears on the formulation of policy. It is the purpose of the series to make the findings of this research available to those who are responsible for raising a new generation and for shaping policy in its behalf. We hope that these books will provide rich and useful information for parents, educators, child-care professionals, students of developmental psychology, and all others concerned with the challenge of human growth.

Jerome Bruner
New York University

Michael Cole
University of California, San Diego

Annette Karmiloff-Smith
Medical Research Council, London

SERIES EDITORS

The Developing Child Series

Children
Solving
Problems

Stephanie Thornton

Harvard University Press
Cambridge, Massachusetts
London, England
1995

Library of Congress Cataloging-in-Publication Data

Thornton, Stephanie, 1952–
  Children solving problems / Stephanie Thornton.
    p. cm.—(The Developing child)
  Includes bibliographical references and index.
   ISBN 0-674-11623-2 (alk. paper).—ISBN 0-674-11624-0 (pbk.: alk. paper)
   1. Problem solving in children. I. Title. II. Series.
BF723.P8T 1995

155.4′1343—dc20

95-1114
   CIP

Acknowledgments

There are many people to thank for their support in the preparation of this book. Some of the research described in Chapter 4 was supported by grants from the Economic and Social Research Council. The original artwork was created by Katy Bignell. Grateful thanks to the colleagues who read early drafts, particularly Nicola Yuill. And most of all to Jackie Gains, without whose extraordinary efficiency and support I would never have had time to write anything at all. Thanks also to my family—David, Simon, Bill, and Joy—to whom this book is dedicated.

Contents

Children
Solving
Problems

1 / Why Children's Problem-Solving Is Interesting

Simon and James (both eight years old) are playing in the yard. They are pretending to be shipwrecked and are busy building a shelter from the odds and ends they've found lying around—tomato stakes and pieces of clothesline, old sheets, branches of bracken for thatching, and cardboard packaging from a new refrigerator. This sort of play is typical of childhood. It absorbs children in total concentration, creating a glowing excitement and so much enthusiasm that it can be hard to persuade the players to break off to eat or go to bed! And yet the major ingredient in this game—as in a great many others—is problem-solving: figuring out where to start, sizing up which things to use from those available, planning the next step, wrestling with the difficulties of fastening the elements together—and puzzling over what went wrong if the shelter collapses. Play such as this makes it quite obvious that children can really enjoy solving problems.

The fact that children enjoy solving problems is somewhat surprising. By definition, "problem-solving" is what you do when you have a goal and don't know how to achieve it, so we might have expected it to be a rather frustrating and negative experience. Figuring out how to solve a new problem is also a challenging intellectual task, which pushes children to evaluate their own efforts, to discover new concepts, and to invent new strategies. We are used to thinking of those things as work, as being dull and boring rather than fun. But even babies in their cribs enjoy solving problems (how do you get a rattle to make a sound?), which shows just how fundamental the process of solving problems is to our human makeup—and to childhood.

Nevertheless, solving problems *is* hard work, especially for very young children. The younger the child, the smaller the range of problems he or she is likely to solve, and the greater the effort involved. Very young babies may spend hours trying to get their thumbs into their mouths—and stabbing their foreheads and noses as they misjudge—though this task is no longer a problem for the six-month-old. The effort to balance three blocks, one on top of the other, can baffle—and amuse—a one-year-old, but it is mundane for an older sibling. Preschoolers can easily solve many problems quite beyond the scope of the one-year-old, but they are defeated by a range of puzzles that are easy for the seven- or ten-year-old, such as tying shoe laces, doing basic arithmetic, playing chess, planning a shopping expedition, and so on. Ten-year-olds may impress us with the range of problems they can tackle, from mending complex toys to mastering difficult concepts in school or interpreting subtle social cues. But even at this age, their problem-solving is still immature: few adults, having no boat to row on a pond, would set out in a cardboard box, for example, though such things are no surprise to the parents of a ten-year-old!

The obvious developmental increase in the ability to solve problems is a puzzle. Does it come from basic changes in mental skills—in the very ability to reason—as the child grows older? If so, how exactly do these skills change? Or is it more a matter of practice, of learning to apply skills successfully in new contexts? Just what do children do when they try to solve problems and how do they get better at it?

The Process of Solving Problems

This book is not about how to improve a child's problem-solving (although we shall come back to that in Chapter 5). Rather, it is about the process of solving problems and the way in which this process develops through childhood.

How can we explore the motivations and the mental processes children bring to problem-solving? How can we find out, for example, how James decided to thatch his shelter with bracken instead of grass or leaves, or how Simon thought of the idea of weaving bracken stems together so they wouldn't slide off the roof? How can we discover what made these two boys work at their task for six hours, when the mere suggestion of homework or tidying up their rooms would cause instant exhaustion?

We can't actually see the mental processes and motivations involved in solving problems. We can only make inferences about what is in the child's mind. Nevertheless, we sometimes get the feeling that we can literally see children thinking from the concentration on their faces or the quizzical expression in their eyes. With a child we know well, we may sometimes have the feeling that we know just what that child is thinking, too! But this is only an illusion. All we see is the outward behavior, not the mental process or motive that produced it. There is almost always more than one interpretation of what we see. Most parents know that a look of concentration in an infant sometimes means fascination with a new discovery, but just as often, it may mean that the infant is filling its diaper! Equally, one may congratulate a group of children on the raft they have built, only to be witheringly told that it is not a raft but a space station, and not a rudder one is leaning against but a nuclear reactor. And what teacher has not wondered, at one time or another, whether the child staring into space at the back of the room is daydreaming or thinking about what to write next?

Nonetheless, there are ways of interpreting what we see as children solve problems, and of testing how good our interpretation is. By using all sorts of clues, from the mistakes children make to the patterns of their successes and failures, from listening to what they tell us themselves to analyzing the detail of their actions, we can form theories about the development of problem-solving. We can test those theories by seeing if they predict what children will do in a new situation or by exploring how computer simulations of these theories behave. As the research I describe here will show, improvements in the tools we use to study children's problem-solving are leading to a new understanding of how these skills develop.

Themes and Organization

One major theme of the work surveyed here is that solving a problem does not depend on being very smart or on difficult and abstract kinds of reasoning, such as logic, as we often assume. The idea that logic is the critical element in problem-solving has been a key part of some influential theories, including that of Jean Piaget.[1] But there is a growing body of evidence that the young child's difficulties in solving problems have little to do with weak logical skills and that even adults rarely reason in abstract or logical ways, as we shall see in Chapter 2. Chapter 3 shows how problem-solving skills grow out of the ordinary process of understanding the world around us, of discovering and using information, and of reacting to and interpreting the feedback provided by our activities.

A second theme is that problem-solving is about change, about moving from one idea to another, new one. Inventing a new solution to a problem is a highly creative process. Children invent new strategies as they interact with a problem. The research described in Chapter 4 shows how the details of children's experience in a task and the feedback they get from their actions play a crucial role in shaping what they do or do not discover.

The third theme is that problem-solving is anything but a dry, intellectual activity. As Chapter 5 shows, the child's increasing success in solving problems is a social process much more bound up in feelings than we used to think: confidence can be more important than skill. The reasons we address a problem have a huge impact on whether or not we solve it successfully. Just as the Russian psychologist Lev Vygotsky proposed, problem-solving is a social skill learned in social interactions in the context of everyday activities.[2] It is much more malleable, and more teachable, than we supposed.

If we draw all these themes together, the process of solving problems emerges as a central part of our everyday lives. To understand problem-solving is to shed light not only on the nature of human intelligence as a whole, but on the very heart of human imagination.

2 / A Historical Perspective on Children's Problem-Solving: Inference and the Development of Logic

Considering how vital a part problem-solving plays in children's lives, in their games and in their struggles to master the challenges of their physical, social, and educational worlds, it is surprising that the topic has so often been treated as simply another facet of cognitive development as a whole, rather than as an issue in its own right. Researchers and educators alike have assumed that children's success in solving problems is just a reflection of the caliber or maturity of their cognitive skills: if we understand how cognitive skills develop, we shall understand childhood problem-solving.

Problem-solving involves processes over and above a child's basic cognitive competence. But there is a sense in which the historical assumption is quite right: we cannot hope to understand children's problem-solving unless we know something about their basic cognitive skills. In this chapter and the next, I shall explore the development of children's cognitive tools and the effects of this development on their ability to solve problems. I shall start by looking at the themes and assumptions that have traditionally shaped how we think about the development of problem-solving. Modern ideas are easier to grasp in this historical context.

The Idea of General Skills

One strong traditional idea about cognitive skills is that they are very general. That is to say, the same basic skills apply in all contexts and to all types of tasks or problems. We can see this idea in many of the different approaches to understanding thinking, from the idea of "general" intelligence to efforts to write intelligent computer programs. Whenever we say things like "younger children are worse at problem-solving than their elders" or "Mary is better at solving problems than Jane," we are making the same kind of assumption. We are speaking as if the ability to solve problems were a trait (like being shy, for example) that will remain constant, for a given individual, from one situation to another.

The notion that cognitive skills are very general has several attractions. First, it makes the task of understanding things like problem-solving seem much easier: if the same skills are involved in all types of problem-solving, then we can study these skills in only one or two contexts rather than having to study problem-solving across a large number of situations. Second, it makes the task of teaching children to reason seem easier: if we teach children to reason in one type of task, we can expect them to carry the cognitive skills over into other tasks too (this assumption underlies the old view that learning Latin provides a general training for the mind, and the newer view that learning computer programming can do the same). Third, using the same skills in all situations seems to make sense from a "design" perspective: it is more economical, and more flexible, than having different skills for different types of task.

General Skills in Problem-Solving: Inference

It is easy to identify general skills in problem-solving at several levels, as we can see from looking at an example. Mary (aged seven) is trying to do a jigsaw puzzle. She fits the pieces together, copying the picture on the box. But when she has used all the pieces, there is still an empty spot. Now she has a new problem: where is the missing piece? She looks in the box and then under the table, but it isn't in either place. After hesitating a bit, she goes off to look in the toy chest.

We can describe what Mary is doing in various ways. For example, we can break what happened down into a number of different steps: *recognizing* that there is a problem and *identifying* a new goal (finding the missing piece of the puzzle); *planning* a strategy to fix the problem; *noticing* whether or not this strategy works and planning another one if it does not.

Almost every instance of problem-solving can be broken down into these same general steps. Each step has its own character, but all have something in common that points to an even more general skill underlying all aspects of problem-solving: at each step, the child must make sense of the information available and use that information to generate a new understanding of the problem or a new strategy. Very often this involves what Jerome Bruner has called "going beyond the information given."[1] That is to say, it involves making *inferences* or *deductions* that take the child from what he or she originally knew to some new piece of information or new idea. For Mary, it is deducing that the jigsaw puzzle has a piece missing from the fact that there is still a gap when all the pieces at hand have been used.

Of course, inferences are a key element in any cognitive process, not just problem-solving. Knowing how children draw inferences would provide us with powerful insights into most aspects of their intelligence.

A General Inference Mechanism: Logic

What sort of mental process could a child use to draw inferences? If we start from the assumption that the process is very general, then we must look for inference mechanisms that would work equally well in any situation. In other words, we must look for an abstract sort of process that does not rely on particular information or details in the problem to which it is applied. The best candidate seems to be logic.

Logic was devised by the ancient Greek philosophers precisely in order to form the principles of "correct" reasoning or inference. There are many different kinds of logic, but they all share the same basic feature: each provides a system for drawing inferences, for extrapolating from some initial information to reach a new conclusion. Each does this in an abstract way, quite independent of the context in which it is used. It is worth looking at this last point quite closely, as it will be important to my argument later on. Here is a logical "argument":

(1) Only literate people can read books.
(2) You are reading this book.
(3) I can therefore infer [the new information] that you must be literate.

In this example, the conclusion is obviously true. That is to say, it is factually accurate. It is also logically valid: the conclusion (3) follows from the premises (1) and (2). But logical validity and factual accuracy are not the same thing. An argument can be logically valid but not factually accurate, as in this example:

(1) If it rains in Poland, pigs dance in Scotland.
(2) It is raining in Poland.
(3) So pigs are dancing in Scotland.

All that matters in logic is the *form* of the argument, not the meaning of the premises or the conclusion. The form of the argument here is:

(1) If A is true, then B is true.
(2) A is true.
(3) So B must be true.

From a logical point of view, it does not matter what A and B are—they could be anything. The inference is valid because it follows the rules of logic, and these same rules apply in every context. It is this property that makes logic seem such a general tool for problem-solving.

Are Children Less Logical Than Adults?

Logic has been accepted as the basis for mature reasoning for the best part of two thousand years. In that context, an obvious explanation of the young child's relatively poor problem-solving performance is that young children are not as good at logical reasoning as their elders. This theory was most convincingly and coherently put forward by Jean Piaget, whose work dominated developmental research through the middle part of this century.[2]

Piaget studied children's reasoning from birth to adolescence. He believed that the root cause of the changes we see in children's problem-solving throughout their development was the gradual growth of logical structures and skills from next to nothing at birth through a succession of stages to the sophisticated logic of the adult. Margaret Donaldson provides an excellent sum-mary of Piaget's theory in the appendix to her book *Children's Minds*.[3] For the purpose of the argument here, the key idea is that, at each stage, the child's reasoning is characterized by a certain level of logical skill, which is fairly constant across different kinds of tasks. Piaget argued that one can predict which problems children will solve and which they will fail to solve on the basis of the stage of logical development they have reached. He provided many illustrations to support this prediction throughout childhood. Let's look at two familiar examples.

In the first (the *class inclusion* task) the experimenter asks a child to look at a collection of birds like that shown in Figure 1. The experimenter then asks: "Are there more ducks or more birds?" Piaget argued that children under the age of seven or eight would be unable to answer this question correctly, because they do not yet have the mental structures to allow them to realize that something can be a member of two classes at the same time. They therefore cannot make the logical inference that, because the ducks are included in the class "birds," there *must* be more birds than ducks. And indeed, whereas a child of eight or nine will confidently answer that there are more birds, most four-year-olds will say that there are more ducks. This mistake is striking, especially as, in other contexts, four-year-olds are quite able to say that ducks are birds.

In the second example (the *transitivity* task) the child is shown two sticks—a red one and a blue one. The red stick is shorter than the blue one. The experimenter hides the red stick and then shows the child the blue stick and a new green stick. The blue stick is shorter than the green stick. The child is then asked: "Which is shorter, the red stick or the green one?" A child of eight or more will have no difficulty in answering this question—the red

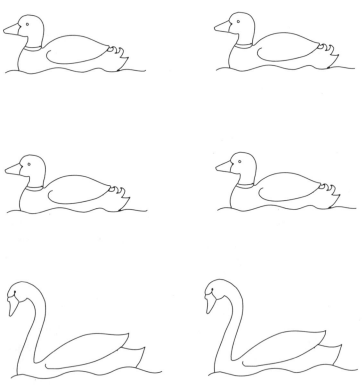

Figure 1

stick is the shortest (see Figure 2). But children under the age of six or seven will have problems; they may say, for example, that they cannot tell, since they have not seen the two sticks together. Again, these young children fail to draw what seems to an adult eye to be a straightforward and obvious inference. Piaget argued that this is because the younger child has not yet developed the mental structures necessary to recognize that a stick can be longer than some things and shorter than others at one and the same time, and so cannot draw the appropriate logical inference.

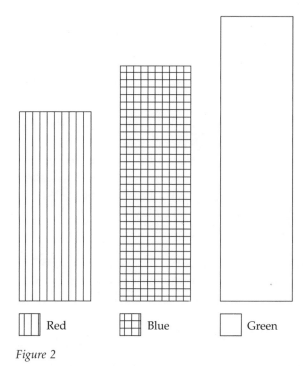

Figure 2

Piaget's experiments are very easy to repeat. If we do just what he did, we will get the same results. Piaget's theory is still very influential, but there is mounting evidence that it is wrong.

Children's Inferences

Despite the fact that they so readily fail in Piaget's tasks, it is clear that even very young children can draw quite sophisticated inferences in some contexts. The evidence for this is all around us, though we seldom realize its significance. For example, here is an interchange between a mother and child of about two:

Child (very aggrieved):	Jack broke my car!
Mother:	I'm sure he didn't . . .
Child:	He did! He did! Harry didn't go there [the playroom]—Jack broke my car!

The interesting point in this accusation is the clear and surprisingly complex chain of inference it involves: if the car is broken, then someone must have done something to it to break it; if someone broke the car, then they must have been in the playroom (where the car was) at the time. If Jack went into the playroom and Harry didn't, then only Jack could have broken the car, so he is the main suspect.

How can it be that a two-year-old is able to put this chain of inferences together but a seven-year-old is unable to draw the right conclusion in Piaget's tasks? The answer seems to be that Piaget's tasks are not the best measures of children's ability to draw inferences.

Piaget deliberately avoided using familiar situations in designing his experimental tasks, because he wanted to test children's ability to reason, not what they might have learned from experience. In her influential book *Children's Minds*, Margaret Donaldson made an important observation about this policy: problem-solving is much harder in unfamiliar situations than it is in familiar ones, even for an adult.[4] This is true even where the familiar problem and the unfamiliar one ought to involve exactly the same logical problem. Part of what we mean when we say that a given type of problem is familiar is that we recognize what to do in that situation—we know which mental tools to use, how and where to look for a solution. We know what the solution is supposed to look like. In unfamiliar situations, we have to work all this out and may fail to solve the problem not because we cannot solve it but because we have failed to recognize what was needed. Donaldson argued that by measuring children's ability to draw logical inferences in unfamiliar tasks, Piaget used too hard a test. His research strategy in designing problem-solving tasks led him to underestimate the young child's ability to draw logical inferences.

Donaldson also pointed out that many of Piaget's tasks are a little strange: for example, "Are there more ducks or more birds?" is a silly question if you understand that a duck *is* a bird. Adults know that psychologists (and teachers) often ask bizarre questions for their own abstruse purposes, but young children are not yet worldly enough to understand this. They are also used to seeing adults as wiser and more knowledgeable. Donaldson argued that children faced with an apparently silly question assume that the adult is actually asking something sensible. They then try to do the intelligent thing—they try to work out what the questioner might have meant and answer *that* question, rather than the one that was actually asked. In the class inclusion task, the obvious "sensible" question would be: "Are there more ducks or more *other* birds?" Answering this question would lead the child to the usual error, even though the child might be perfectly capable of drawing a proper logical inference in another situation.

Many researchers have demonstrated that very young children can be much more successful in drawing inferences than their performance in Piaget's tasks suggests. Rochel Gelman's review of a number of studies shows that young children can often solve problems when they are couched in concrete, familiar, everyday terms, even though they fail with the very same problems when they are expressed abstractly or in an unfamiliar way.[5]

The impact of the way a problem is expressed is easy

to illustrate. Not many two- or three-year-olds would successfully cope with this abstract problem:

(1) If A is true, then B is true.
(2) A is true.
    What follows?

But very few would have any trouble with this more concrete version, even though it involves exactly the same form of inference:

(1) If you're good on the shopping trip, you can have an ice cream cone.
(2) You were good on the shopping trip.
    What follows?

The fact that children's success in logical problem-solving seems to vary from one context to another strongly challenges Piaget's theory of developmental stages and his interpretation of the nature of children's difficulties in his original studies. Researchers like Donaldson have argued that if a child can successfully solve a logical problem in even one context, it must be that that child *does* have the requisite logical skills.[6] If that child fails to solve the same problem in another context, the difficulty must be related to something *other* than logical skill per se. For psychologists such as Donaldson, changes in children's problem-solving success require an explanation quite different from Piaget's account of the growth of logical skills.

Of course, Piaget's supporters countered this approach by challenging the claim that very young children had used logical skills to succeed in the new versions of the tasks. The fact that two versions of a task have the same logical *structure* does not necessarily mean that people will use the same logical *processes* in solving them both. One version of a task, for example, might compel the child to draw a logical inference, while another version might allow the problem to be solved from memory or by using situational cues. Any task can be completed through a variety of different processes. Just because a problem can be described in terms of a specific kind of logical inference need not mean that someone solving the problem must actually make that inference to succeed. The correct answer can be obtained in another way.

Resolving a controversy like this one is quite difficult. As we saw in Chapter 1, it is not possible to see the process by which a child tackles a task directly. One can only draw inferences about it on the basis of the evidence from the child's behavior. Where two opposing theories clearly predict different patterns of behavior, we can look to see which makes the most accurate predictions. But where the two theories set out to explain the same behavior in contrasting ways, it is quite difficult to identify different predictions to test.

Happily, the controversy about whether very young children do or do not use logic in solving particular versions of Piaget's tasks is the least important issue emerging from this line of research. Much more exciting is the discovery that children's success in problem-solving varies from one situation to another, even where successive situations apparently involve the same logical skill. Now, if level of logical skill were the *main factor* in problem-solving, we would not expect to see this kind of variation between different versions of a task. Low logical skill should mean consistent failure, and high logical skill consistent success in tasks with the same logical structure. The fact that children's performance is *not* consistent across different versions of a task clearly implies that *logical skill is not the main factor underlying the child's success or failure in problem-solving*. Other factors must be involved and must play a more critical role in the development of problem-solving skill—either in constraining when a child can use logical skills or in determining when a child can solve a problem despite the absence of logical skills.

Furthermore, the fact that children's success is not consistent, even from one version of a task to another, undermines the whole idea that general skills are the key to problem-solving: obviously, factors specific to particular tasks and situations are at least as important.

Adults and Logical Reasoning

Are adults any more reliant on general abstract skills such as logic than children? Coincidentally, just as studies of children's inference are showing that factors other than logical skills determine the child's success or failure in problem-solving, research is also finding that logic is less important in adult problem-solving than we have thought. It is worth looking at studies of adult reasoning in some detail, because these studies are radically changing our understanding of what is involved in mature problem-solving, thus shedding new light on children's problem-solving.

The theory that problem-solving depends on very general, abstract logical skills implies that adults, who are good at solving problems, ought to be good at drawing logical inferences. But they aren't. For instance, here are some problems that call for inferences about which class things belong to, somewhat reminiscent of the inferences Piaget explored in the "class inclusion" task.

(1) All ducks are fowl.
(2) All fowl are birds.
(3) Therefore all ducks are birds.

(1) All ducks are fowl.
(2) All fowl are wild.
(3) Therefore all ducks are wild.

(1) All ducks are swimmers.
(2) Some swimmers have webbed feet.
(3) Therefore all ducks have webbed feet.

Which, if any, of the conclusions above are logically valid? A study by Jonathan Evans and his colleagues shows that 90 percent of adults will recognize that a logical argument is valid if the premises and the conclusion are also factually accurate, as in the first example above. But only 46 percent can recognize that the conclusion is logically valid when it is factually inaccurate, as in the second example. Even fewer realize that a conclusion is *not* logically valid when both the premises and the conclusion are factually accurate, as in the third example.[7]

Effects of this kind are called "belief bias" effects. What they show is that even adults have enormous difficulty in applying logical principles. They prefer to draw on their prior knowledge about the real world and have great difficulty putting that knowledge aside in order to think logically.

Of course, there are logical problems that adults seem to find much easier than children do. Adults, for example, are very good at solving the kinds of transitive inference problem that young children find so difficult. But studies of *how* they solve such problems do not support Piaget's assumptions that adults actually use *logical* inferences.

This conclusion comes from studies by George Potts and others that have looked at how adults solve Piaget's transitive inference problems when there are not three, but six elements to be compared:[8]

(1) Tom is taller than Dick.
(2) Dick is taller than Sam.
(3) Sam is taller than Pete.

(4) Pete is taller than Jack.
(5) Jack is taller than Joe.

Making comparisons between boys who are far apart in this list ought to involve more inferences than would be needed to make comparisons between boys who are closer together. For example, to infer that Dick is taller than Pete, one need make only one transitive inference:

(1) Dick is taller than Sam.
(2) Sam is taller than Pete.
(3) Therefore Dick is taller than Pete.

But to infer that Dick is taller than Joe, one ought to make three transitive inferences:

(1) Dick is taller than Sam.
(2) Sam is taller than Pete.
(3) Therefore Dick is taller than Pete.

(1) Pete is taller than Jack.
(2) Jack is taller than Joe.
(3) Therefore Pete is taller than Joe.

(1) Dick is taller than Pete.
(2) Pete is taller than Joe.
(3) Therefore Dick is taller than Joe.

If we assume that it takes a certain amount of time to draw a transitive inference, it follows that it should take longer to compare Dick and Joe, who are far apart in the series and therefore need three inferences, than it takes to compare Dick and Pete, who are closer and need only one. But this is not what we find.

Potts tested a number of college students on such problems and found that they could make comparisons between elements that are far apart in a series more quickly than they could make comparisons between elements that are close together. But this is exactly the *opposite* of what ought to happen if they were solving the problem solely by logical inferences: how could they make three inferences more quickly than one? We can only conclude that they are not in fact solving the problem by drawing transitive inferences.

This conclusion is reinforced by an even more striking finding. Suppose we ask people to say "true" or "false" to a number of statements, for example: "Dick is taller than Joe." We might expect that they could make such judgments most speedily when the statement is one they were given to learn at the start of the task, and less speedily when the comparison is not one they have previously learned. But we would be wrong! Adults are faster in judging comparisons involving boys far apart in the series (who have not previously been directly compared) than they are in judging comparisons of boys who *are* directly compared in the statements given at the start of the experiment. In other words, judgments that ought to involve several inferences can be made faster than those that should involve no inferences at all. This would be very difficult to understand if adults were actually solving the problem by drawing transitive inferences.

In fact, however, Potts's research suggests that adults solve such problems by building a sort of mental picture of, for example, the heights of the boys, and arranging these into a series from tallest to shortest (see Figure 3). Rather than draw logical inferences about the relative height of two boys, an adult consults this mental model. Studies of how people use actual, visible models to make comparisons show that it is easier to compare items that can be found quickly than those that take more looking for; items toward the ends of a series are easier to find, and thus can be compared more quickly. What this sug-

Tom   Dick   Sam   Pete   Jack   Joe

Figure 3

gests is that the processes by which adults solve transitive inference problems may have more to do with processes for constructing mental models of information than with logic.

There are also clear demonstrations that adults, like children, are more successful with some versions of supposedly logical problems than they are with others. Such effects show that, just as is the case with children, adult problem-solving must be affected by factors other than logical skill itself. The most famous demonstration of such effects comes from Peter Wason and Philip Johnson-Laird's studies of tasks supposed to measure inferences about situations in which one thing is dependent on another.[9] Such reasoning is called *conditional reasoning.* Wason and Johnson-Laird studied two examples of conditional reasoning tasks that draw on exactly the same logical inference. The first is an abstract version of the problem (see Figure 4):

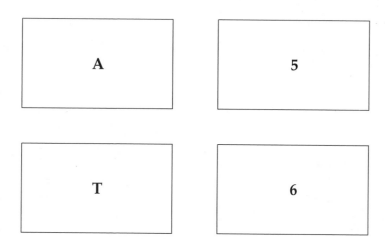

Figure 4

> If a card has a vowel on one side, then it has an even number on the other side. Which cards must you turn over to check whether the rule is true?

The second is a more concrete version of the same problem (see Figure 5):

> If an envelope is sealed, then it has a five-penny stamp on it. Which envelopes must you turn over to check whether the rule is true?

Only 8 percent of college students draw the right inferences and solve the abstract version of the problem correctly. Almost all realize that you should turn over the card showing a vowel to check that it has an even number on the back. Some suggested that you should also turn over the card showing an even number to check that it has a vowel on the back. In fact, this is wrong: if we look carefully at the rule, we can see that it does not say that even numbers can *only* be paired with vowels, just that vowels can only be paired with even numbers. Al-

Figure 5

most no one thought of testing the rule by checking on the odd number to make sure there is no vowel behind it.

By contrast, 87 percent of adults can successfully solve the more concrete version of the task, provided that they have had previous experience of this kind of postal rule, as most English people in the 1970s did. American subjects and younger English ones who have not experienced the rule have much more difficulty. This seems to suggest that adults need specific, relevant information and experience with the task to cope with this kind of inference—but that is not quite right. It is not so much the concrete experience of the postal rule that matters but whether or not the rule seems to "make sense." Providing a rationale, an explanation for the postal rule, made the more concrete version of the task easier, even for people who had no direct experience of the postal rule itself.[10] Understanding the rationale seems to allow us to integrate a particular rule with our general knowledge about rules and regulations.

We all learn a lot about how to follow regulations. Many have the same basic form as the postal rule: the appropriate course of action (such as sealing or not sealing an envelope) depends on the circumstances (such as the value of the stamp used). We have learned to check that the circumstances are right for taking the action *and* for not taking it. It is as if our experience has given us a special "recipe" for checking on conditional rules, which can stand in for the processes of logical inference that would otherwise be needed.

Overall, logic is far less relevant even to adult problem-solving than we thought. Forced to think logically, we make mistakes and find the problem hard. In tasks that ought to involve logical inferences, the evidence suggests that we do not in fact use logical processes even though we can draw the inferences. Even professional logicians do not generally use logic in the everyday contexts where that would be the most obvious and appropriate thing to do. Just like children, we adults are more likely to draw on factual knowledge than on logic, and our success is more influenced by factors particular to the task in hand than by any consistent general skill.

The Development of Logical Skill

Of course, it is obvious that human beings can *sometimes* draw strictly logical inferences in solving problems. If this were not so, we would not have been able to develop, or understand, formal models of logic at all. Even if logic is not the fundamental element in problem-solving, the question of how the ability to use logic develops is still interesting and must be answered.

First, what is it that develops as we become more adept at drawing and understanding logical inferences? Do we really ever develop strictly "logical" mental processes? In view of the results from studies of adult reasoning, some researchers, such as Philip Johnson-Laird, have argued that we do not.[11] They take the view that logical inferences are never produced by "logical" processes at all, but by other types of psychological process. For example, Johnson-Laird has suggested that these other processes involve drawing inferences from mental models (much as in Potts's study of reasoning about series described above).

At first it seems absurd to say that logical problem-solving does not involve logical mental processes. But there is nothing contradictory in this. There is no reason why a process should resemble the product it produces. For example, a fire produces ash, but its flames do not resemble the ash in any way. A process (such as combustion) need not share any structural property with the product (the ash) it creates. It is not necessary for logical inferences to be produced by a process with the structural properties of logic.

If Johnson-Laird is right, then the development of logical reasoning has to be understood in terms of the development of the ability to create and use mental models. There is enough evidence supporting this theory to make this a very plausible thesis in studies with both adults and children. For example, the ability to solve syllogistic problems emerges around the age of nine to twelve years. Johnson-Laird and his associates have shown that children of this age solve syllogisms by building mental models of the relationships between classes and "reading off" the correct inferences from these models.[12] They found no evidence that more explicitly logical processes were involved. Equally, Jerome Bruner and Helen Kenney found that children of eight to ten begin to solve mathematical problems by devising concrete mental models of the task.[13] Yet this makes it difficult for them to recognize analogies between problems that share the same abstract structure but have different concrete details. Working through many similar problems, however, allowed the children to gradually build up a "composite" mental image combining all the separate, specific images. This not only enabled them to achieve a more abstract grasp of the problem, it also freed them to generalize across different examples of that type of task and to begin to understand its formal properties. But the abstract representation remained rooted in the concrete mental models from which it had come: the children's "stock of imagery" about the problem continued to play an important role in actually addressing it.

Whatever the psychological *process* underlying the use of formal logical inferences, it is plain that the tendency to draw such inferences develops throughout childhood. Study after study shows that, in at least some situations, even very young children can draw certain types of logical inference—markedly more than Piaget thought. But the younger the child, the narrower the range of contexts in which this is the case and the simpler the inferences he or she can draw.

Although there are many things about this developmental progression that we do not yet understand, some are becoming clearer. For example, logic is very closely related to language. Logical analysis depends on following through the exact meanings of words like *if, and, unless, or,* and so on. These words are used much more precisely and more formally in logic than they are in ordinary speech. Nevertheless, it may well be that the infant first begins to make simple logical inferences by learning to use these words in a natural human language.

Margaret Donaldson argues that the business of understanding language may also explain both the young child's rather limited and erratic use of logical inferences and the older child's ability to draw logical conclusions in a more explicit way.[14] She has pointed out that we have two different modes for understanding language. Ordinary, everyday understanding is not based very precisely on the actual words used: we focus on the meaning the speaker intends to convey rather than the literal meaning of what the speaker actually says. Analytic understanding is just the opposite: it focuses on literal meanings rather than intentions. A friend of mine was very fond of an irritating joke that brings out this distinction very clearly: He would set up opportunities in restaurants for others to say "Could you pass the salt?" to which he would reply "Yes!" but would not do so. The victim of this riposte would then demand the salt, insisting that the ordinary interpretation of the original request quite obviously implied that he or she wanted the salt and had asked for it to be passed over. My friend would answer that the literal (that is analytic) meaning of the words was no such thing. He had merely been asked whether he was *capable* of passing the salt—to which he thought he had given a fully adequate response!

Donaldson and other researchers are exploring the ways in which these different usages of language affect logical reasoning. Ordinary, everyday language supports some kinds of logical inference in the day-to-day situations in which it is relevant. So the everyday use of language allows even very young children to handle quite complex conditional inferences ("If you don't sit down and eat, I shall be very angry!") in the course of their everyday activities. By contrast, the ability to articulate a logical principle, to handle logic in abstract ways, and to transfer logical principles from one situation to another requires an analytical appreciation of language. To master logic in the abstract, one must interpret the strict meanings of words without reference either to their context or to the motives or purposes of ordinary activities. This is hard to do, and it involves an approach quite different from the normal process of using language in context. Some individuals never master complex abstract logical inferences at all. There is striking evidence that learning to read plays a key role in developing the ability to process language analytically, and thus, in developing explicit logical skills. The beginning reader must pay attention to the literal words on the page, learn to recognize alternative meanings, and decide which meaning is intended in a given sentence. This in turn fosters the reflective approach to the meaning of words that is the essence of an analytical approach to language. Certainly, classic studies by Alexander Luria, and by Michael Cole and Sylvia Scribner have shown that formal schooling and interaction with a literate society have a major influence on the development of such skills.[15]

But the ability to draw a logical inference by no means ensures that a child (or an adult, for that matter) will actually draw that inference, even in everyday contexts where ordinary language might support logic. A study by Jan Hawkins and others[16] found that four- and five-year-old children could make certain logically correct deductions—and even justify them—when dealing with fantasy situations, but they were less reliable when dealing with familiar, everyday ones! The difficulty appears to relate to the problem of choosing between logical validity and factual accuracy. In fantasy situations, the child has no practical experience to fall back on, no yardstick of what is factually accurate. There is nothing, therefore, to divert reasoning from the logical. But in familiar situations, logical validity is sometimes in conflict with factual accuracy. In such situations, young children and adults alike are prone to abandon logic and base their responses on what they know to be true. Older individuals are more able to resist this tendency where it is appropriate to do so and more able to recognize when it *is* appropriate. Logic is only one of the strategies available to the problem-solver, and it is not necessarily the preferred approach, even where it would be the most effective one.

A New View of Problem-Solving Processes

The traditional emphasis on general skills such as logic has made us look at problem-solving in a very abstract way: because logic is a general basis for reasoning, it is as appropriate, in principle, to a Martian or any other intelligent entity as to a human being. According to this view, there is therefore nothing specifically human about problem-solving. Because logic exists outside the context of any particular activity, it ignores the content and meaning of the material to which it is applied. Content and meaning therefore have no role to play in problem-solving processes. Furthermore, Piaget's "logical" problem-solver, constructing his or her own mental processes, seems to exist more or less outside the context of the species or culture to which he or she belongs.

The research reviewed in this chapter reveals a completely different view of what is involved in problem-solving. Logic, and general skills as a whole, are less important to the process of solving problems than we thought. Other factors, which vary from one situation to another, play a major role in determining whether a child—or an adult—will be able to solve a problem. Logic itself is just one of a range of strategies for approaching a problem. Whether and when we develop the ability to use a logical strategy depends on specifically human developments, such as language, and on the social practices of formal schooling. And even when we do choose a logical strategy, we may be invoking not abstract logical processes but rather human, psychological ones, such as building mental models of what we know. The content and the meaning of the problem determine how we approach it.

3 / Conceptual Tools for Solving Problems: Inherent Skills and Information

Human problem-solving depends on psychological processes. In this chapter, we shall see that newborn infants are far from helpless in solving problems. In fact, they start out with a surprising range of skills. Processes necessary for beginning to interpret the world and draw everyday inferences are part of a baby's basic endowment. Unlike logic, many of these processes depend on detailed information about the world. Everyday inference processes extrapolate from experience, so that two children using the same process may draw quite different conclusions if they call on different experiences. The richer information children gather as they gain experience creates new tools for problem-solving: it provides new strategies for a given problem; it promotes new ways of understanding concepts and drawing inferences; and it broadens the possibilities for drawing helpful analogies between one problem and another. The richer the child's information, the easier it is for the child to plan just how to tackle a problem.

Inherent Skills

Psychologists used to believe that newborn babies had very limited skills for solving problems. This idea was reinforced by Jean Piaget, who believed that babies are born with no more than a few simple reflexes, and by earlier writers such as John Locke, who saw the baby as a blank slate or "tabula rasa."[1] But in fact, even newborns have a surprising range of abilities and can cope quite well with various complex concepts.

For example, from birth babies have at least a rudimentary conception of number. In one study, Karen Wynn put a mouse where a baby could see it and then blocked off the view with a screen. If she secretly added another mouse before she removed the screen, the baby showed surprise, revealing an awareness of a change in the number of mice.[2] In addition, right from birth, babies are predisposed to distinguish between the animate and the inanimate using such cues as whether something can move under its own steam, as a biological being would, or whether it relies on other agencies to move, as inanimate objects do.[3] Even the basis of language, which will play an important role in the development of problem-solving, as we have begun to see in Chapter 2, is already present at birth. Jacques Mehler and his colleagues have found that babies can tell the difference between speech and other sounds within twelve hours of birth; at four days old they can tell the difference between one language and another.[4] Mehler found that French babies respond differently to French and Russian, even when they hear the same person speaking both languages.

More striking still, babies are born with the ability to draw certain kinds of inference. Very young babies, for example, can make quite complicated inferences about the things they see. Elizabeth Spelke has found that babies as young as four months can infer that an object (shown in Figure 6) is a block with a solid pole behind it if they see the "pole" move back and forth behind the block.[5] By the age of seven months, babies make this

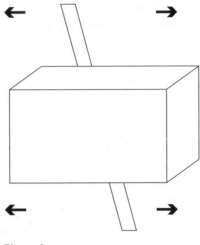

Figure 6

inference whether or not the pole moves, just as an adult would do.

And right from birth, babies can recognize similarities between things and recall past events, although these are quite complex processes. *Without* such basic skills, the infant could not learn and develop. *With* them, the baby is equipped with some surprisingly general tools for drawing inferences.

Inferences from Basic Psychological Processes

The way that we use our inherent ability to recognize similarities or to recall past events as a basis for everyday inferences was first explored by Daniel Kahneman and his associates in trying to explain why adult reasoning is sometimes apparently illogical and biased.[6]

For instance, many people think that flying is more dangerous than driving, although the reverse is actually true. Kahneman explains this in terms of the way we naturally draw everyday inferences based on what we can recall. In general, familiar, common, or likely events are easier to bring to mind than rare or unfamiliar ones (it's easier to remember what your bedroom looks like than to remember a room in a house you visited only once). People tend to ignore the fact that this principle of memory does not always hold true: rare events can be very vivid and memorable, while common events can be so mundane as to be difficult to recall. Yet it is normally safe to assume that common things are more memorable than rare ones and, to invert this principle, to infer that if an event is easily brought to mind, then it must be more common than other events that are harder to bring to mind. Only where the vividness of events (such as the horror of a major plane crash) makes rare things more memorable than common ones (like car accidents, which seem more mundane—unless they are personally experienced) does the principle lead to the wrong conclusion.

Equally, people tend to make inferences on the basis of stereotypes, disregarding other kinds of information. Told only that there are a hundred people in a room, seventy of them lawyers and thirty engineers, people correctly deduce that any one individual coming out of the room is more likely to be a lawyer than an engineer. But the minute they are given any information at all about a specific individual, they disregard the prior odds and base their judgment entirely on how closely that individual fits their stereotype of a lawyer or an engineer. So they infer, for instance, that an individual who sounds like the stereotype of an engineer *is* an engineer, even though, given the odds, it is more likely that he is a lawyer.[7] Kahneman argues that this way of drawing inferences is an extrapolation from the normal way we recognize similarities. Eleanor Rosch has shown that the more something resembles our conception of a stereotypical member of some category, the more likely we are to accept that it is a member of that category and to assume that it has all of the attributes and properties of members of that category.[8] (So, for example, most people are more confident that the Labrador shown at the top of Figure 7 is a dog than that the Portuguese Water Dog or the Chinese Crested Dog are. The Labrador is closer to our stereotype of a dog, and we are more confident that it will behave like a dog—chew slippers, chase cats, and so on—than that the other two will.) As with inferences from recall, it is normally appropriate to infer that things that *look* alike *are* alike. But in some instances, inferences of this kind lead to problems (as anyone who has mistaken a poisonous mushroom for an edible one could tell you!).

There is every reason to suppose that even very young children draw inferences from similarities and from what they can recall, just as adults do. Kahneman believes that the tendency to draw such inferences is unconscious and even unavoidable in certain circumstances.[9] Certainly, drawing inferences in this way is the natural thing to do: it is natural to assume that two things that look alike are alike, and to base judgments on information we can bring to mind, rather than on anything else. Human babies have all the requisite subskills for drawing inferences in this way. In fact, the same is true for animals such as rats and chickens. And indeed, experimental studies confirm that even very young children can draw inferences through these kinds of processes.

Kahneman and his associates have also shown that adults often use simple inference processes where they should use more formal or sophisticated processes based on mathematics or logic. Some theorists, such as Lee Ross, have suggested that children ought to use these processes even more extensively than adults do. Young children are less likely to know about the more sophis-

Figure 7

ticated strategy or to be able to inhibit the automatic everyday inference process.[10] Yet, the evidence does not entirely support this prediction. My studies of inference processes regularly find that children aged eight and older often use recall to draw everyday inferences in the same situations as adults do but are more prone to abandon inference and resort to guessing. Children aged six and younger will spontaneously draw inferences from recall in those situations they find personally motivating or when they are cued to do so, but otherwise they rely much more on guessing. It is not yet clear why this is so. Are younger children less confident about their inferences and so, more likely to disregard them? Or do they less often recognize when inference, as opposed to guessing, is appropriate? Knowing how to assess your skills and when to use them is an important part of developing a facility in problem-solving.

When both adult and child use simple everyday inference processes in tackling a problem, should we expect them to come up with the same conclusions more often than they seem to? The answer is no. An essential aspect of everyday inference processes is that they depend on the information the individual already has. They are, in effect, devices for extrapolating from experience. Younger children have less—and often different—experience of the world than older children or adults. For example, a young adolescent who has had a number of memorable close calls while crossing roads may view traffic as much more dangerous than does the toddler, who has no such experience to draw on. A two-year-old recognizes fewer stereotypes and has less experience to recall than a six-year-old, and so on. Two individuals using the same everyday inference process will reach different conclusions, if they draw on different experiences.

Analyses of everyday inference processes challenge

some traditional assumptions about the development of problem-solving through childhood. Theorists like Jean Piaget emphasized the importance of changes in children's mental tools (such as the development of logic) in explaining why younger children approach problems differently from older children.[11] With everyday inference processes, the emphasis is not on changing mental tools but on changes in the specific knowledge to which children apply these tools. How do these two contrasting perspectives fit together? Research is showing that in many areas, children's concrete knowledge of the task at hand is indeed a major determinant of how they set about tackling the problem and whether they succeed. But we are also discovering that changes in this detailed knowledge make a critical contribution to the emergence of new mental tools.

Inferences from Knowledge about the Task

Studies of how children solve various kinds of problems have identified a number of ways in which their concrete understanding of the task affects both the conclusions they draw and the mental tools they use.

Conclusions Reflect Understanding

One of the roles concrete knowledge can play in problem-solving is illustrated by problems that involve a balance scale (see Figure 8): Will the scales balance or will one arm go down? This question produces some very interesting results. Four- and five-year-olds can make accurate predictions for scales A and C, but they get B and D wrong. Nine-year-olds can get problems A and C right, as well as problem B, but they still get problem D wrong. Fourteen-year-olds typically get problems A and B right but are *less* likely to be successful with problem

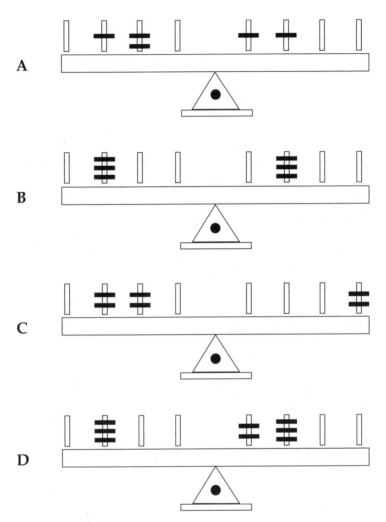

Figure 8

C than the younger children! Only at seventeen are they likely to solve all the problems correctly. Robert Siegler has explained how this curious pattern of results comes about from an expansion in what children have discovered about what makes things balance.[12]

Five-year-olds know that weight matters and that you have to have an equal amount of weight on each arm of the scale to get it to balance. But that's all they know. They get problems A and C right because these problems can be solved simply by taking weight into account. But they are systematically wrong about problems B and D, because here, attending only to weight gives the wrong answer.

Nine-year-olds have discovered that the *position* of weight as well as the *amount* of weight is relevant to balance: further away from the fulcrum is "heavier." But they still don't know how to integrate position and weight, and they use information about position rather selectively. Nine-year-olds look at the weights first. If these are equal, they go on to consider the position of the weights. But if the weights are not equal, they ignore position. So they can successfully solve just those problems the five-year-old can solve *and* those in which weight is equal but position is not (B). But they are still systematically wrong on problem D, because here they attend only to weight.

Fourteen-year-olds know that position must be taken into account as well as weight, but what they do *not* know is how to do it. Their extra understanding actually puts them at a disadvantage: they can solve the problems in which handling weight and position *separately* gives the same answer (A and B), but they do not know what to do when these two cues are in conflict (C and D), so they simply guess. Because they are guessing, they have a fifty-fifty chance of being right, which for problem C gives them a worse chance of success than the five- or nine-year-olds, who are right for the wrong reason. Only seventeen-year-olds have learned enough about the interrelationship between weight and position to take both into account in solving the problems.

Although fourteen-year-olds are less successful than younger children in some versions of the balance problem, their extra knowledge is not entirely a handicap. They know they are only guessing on some of the problems, and they know they need to attend to weight and position in every case: these things put them in a very good position to learn through feedback from the task. In contrast, younger children may simply be mystified about why, in some cases, their answer is wrong, even though they have taken everything that (to them) seems relevant into account. They do not know where the problem lies or what to attend to, and are thus in a weak position to learn from their experience in the task.

In fact, however, by changing what children attend to, we can radically alter what they can learn and what problems they can solve.[13] Five-year-olds learn less from experience with the balance task than eight-year-olds do, which is not surprising: five-year-olds typically do not even notice the position of the weights, much less realize that position is relevant, and they cannot learn anything about the role of position if they do not even notice it. Siegler found that simply by teaching five-year-olds to pay attention to the position of the weights, they were able to learn as much from the task as the eight-year-olds.

Success in solving many problems is less a matter of age than of the information we have and the strategy that information suggests. In the balance scale problem, eight-year-olds can easily be taught to use a strategy that integrates information about weights with information about position. They can then solve balance problems as successfully as seventeen-year-olds.

Understanding Creates New Mental Tools

Acquiring richer concrete knowledge about a task brings children more than new strategies. As Susan Carey has discovered, it can alter the kinds of concepts a child can use and the types of reasoning that are possible.[14] New types of reasoning create new tools for problem-solving.

Carey studied the development of children's understanding of the concept of animacy, and how different degrees of understanding affected their reasoning. As we have seen, even very young babies can differentiate between animate and inanimate things. By the age of three, children usually recognize as alive the same things an adult would: for all their make-believe, three-year-olds do not really expect their dolls, or other inanimate things, to eat or sleep or behave like living creatures. But how young children think about animacy is different in important ways from how older children understand it.

Children four to seven years old do not really understand what a biological entity is or how it functions. If you ask them what is inside their body, they will tell you about the things they have seen going in and out, such as food and blood, but they do not mention the digestive organs or the circulatory system. If you ask them why living things defecate, children of this age might say, for example, that it is to "stop the body from getting too full." If they know they have a heart, they will say that its function is to let you feel things (like love), but they do not mention its role as a pump. They will tell you that a brain is for thinking with but hotly deny that it has anything to do with walking or wiggling your toes.

Because six-year-olds do not understand how bodies work, they do not understand the factors that hold all the members of a category together; that is, they do not have a list of the characteristics that define membership in that category. The only basis on which they can recognize the members of a particular category is through their similarity: they *look* like other members of that category. So, in reasoning about animacy, these children can only draw inferences on the basis of similarities: the more something looks like a typical member of the category, the more confident the child is that it will behave like a member of that category. For children four to seven years old, the most familiar example of a living thing is a human being. Monkeys and dogs look fairly like people, so children of this age believe that they are alive and do the things living creatures do, like eating and breathing and defecating. But rose bushes and trees do not look much like people, so the children infer that these things are not alive and do not behave like living things.

By contrast, most ten-year-old children have gathered a lot more biological information. They know that the brain regulates all bodily functions, and that feeding and defecating are the two end points of a process of digestion, which functions to transform raw materials into building blocks for the body and energy. This additional information does much more than simply enrich children's understanding. It allows them to understand the *definition* of a living thing: to be animate is to be a biological entity; all biological entities share the same problems and solve them in much the same ways; all living things must eat, defecate, and reproduce. Anything that does these things is a biological entity.

When children understand the definition of a given category, they acquire a more sophisticated basis for drawing inferences about the members of that category. They can recognize things as belonging to that category, whatever they look like, and draw inferences from the very fact of category membership, rather than from similarity. Trees and rose bushes can be recognized as animate, even though they are not at all like human beings, our stereotype of living things, because they share the defining properties of a living organism. Reasoning based on category definitions produces different answers than reasoning based on similarity. Category-based reasoning rests on principles and on understanding rather than on extrapolation from simple perceptual processes. And category-based inference is much more useful in formal, analytical reasoning than the fuzzier kind of inference based on similarity.

For the child, having a theory about how things work opens up new avenues for discovery through inference and insight. Moving from a similarity-based to a definition-based concept changes the child's perception of what it is about a category that is important.[15] For a young child relying on similarity to understand the concept "baby," being tiny is a core characteristic. But as soon as children discover that a baby is a "newborn offspring," they realize that size is only a peripheral concomitant: a creature can be huge and still be a baby—a baby whale, for instance. As a child's understanding grows, elements that were at the core of the child's understanding of a concept move to the periphery, and vice versa.

Since the change from a similarity- to a definition-based understanding of concepts is the result of increasing knowledge, the transition occurs at different times for different concepts.[16] A child may have very little information in one area, and so make inferences through similarity in that context, but be very well informed in another area, and so able to draw definition-based inferences in reasoning about that topic. Although three- and four-year-olds have difficulty in making definition-based inferences for complex concepts like animacy, they regularly make such inferences for other concepts that are easier to understand, like "fish." Rochel Gelman and Ellen Markman showed four-year-olds pictures of a tropical fish, a dolphin, and a shark. The dolphin and the shark looked very similar, but the tropical fish and the shark were given the same label ("fish").[17] The children had to decide whether the shark breathed in the same way as the dolphin or in the same way as the tropical fish. These three- and four-year-old children ignored what the creatures looked like and used the category information to infer that the shark breathed like the tropical fish. Even babies as young as a year may be able to draw inferences based on category definitions with some simple concepts.[18]

The transition from similarity-based reasoning to definition-based reasoning is related not to age but to the individual's level of expertise in a particular area. Even adults use similarity-based reasoning in contexts where they have a weak understanding. For example, Michelene Chi found that students beginning a college study of physics tended to group problems that looked similar together and treated them the same way in trying to solve them.[19] Expert physicists, on the other hand, ignore what a problem looks like and group problems together on the basis of the underlying principles involved. The categories recognized by expert and novice physicists can cut right across one another, as Figure 9 shows. For both adults and children, the kinds of concept we use in solving problems and the kinds of inference we can make are heavily dependent on how much information we have and how well we understand the problem.

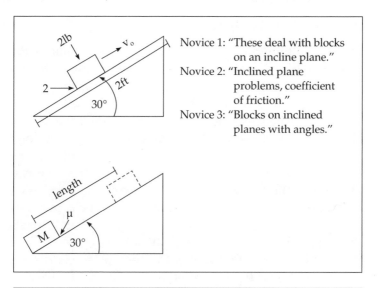

Novice 1: "These deal with blocks on an incline plane."

Novice 2: "Inclined plane problems, coefficient of friction."

Novice 3: "Blocks on inclined planes with angles."

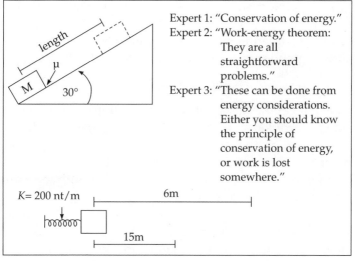

Expert 1: "Conservation of energy."

Expert 2: "Work-energy theorem: They are all straightforward problems."

Expert 3: "These can be done from energy considerations. Either you should know the principle of conservation of energy, or work is lost somewhere."

Figure 9

Using Skills Effectively

Of course, knowledge about the concrete details of the task at hand is not the only kind of knowledge that increases throughout childhood. Children also become more adept at knowing when to use their skills. Sometimes this is because they gradually become more aware of what those skills are, and of how they function. John Flavell and his associates have found that children become increasingly aware of the limitations of human memory and of the need for ruses (like repeating something over and over in order to memorize it) to help memory along.[20] Some researchers believe that such "metacognitive" awareness—that is to say, awareness of one's mental processes—is a key element in the young child's developing ability to deploy skills effectively in solving problems. Nonetheless, it is increasingly clear that concrete knowledge of the task also has an important part to play in creating such metacognitive awareness and in allowing children to deploy their skills effectively.

Drawing Analogies

One important factor in deploying skills effectively in solving problems is the ability to draw analogies. If you can recognize that a new problem is analogous to another problem you already know how to solve, you may be able to solve the new one by tackling it with the same strategies you used for the old one.

Young children are notoriously bad at drawing analogies between one problem and another. Even ten- and eleven-year-olds can be surprisingly poor at this and may need clues to help them find a useful analogy. According to Piaget, this is because one needs fairly sophisticated logical skills to draw analogies[21]—skills that do not develop until eleven or twelve years of age. But new research is showing that the ability to draw analogies depends not so much on logic as on having a rich enough understanding of different situations to be able to recognize a useful analogy.

Let's look at what is involved in drawing analogies:

A bicycle is to handlebars as a ship is to . . . ?

The correct answer is a "rudder." Very few children under ten can answer correctly because few have the right knowledge. The relationship between handlebars and rudders is actually rather esoteric. The two things do not look alike and do not operate in the same way. Their connection is only that each is a steering mechanism. Children with no experience of boats may not realize that they have steering mechanisms, and still less what those mechanisms might be. Young children may not even understand that handlebars steer a bicycle and are not simply something to hold on to.

Studies by Usha Goswami and Ann Brown have found that even very young children can draw analogies when they have enough information about the two areas being compared to be able to recognize the point of analogy.[22] Three-year-olds can often solve such analogies as:

Chocolate is to melted chocolate as snow is to . . . ?

A richer knowledge of a wider range of things means that older children are able to recognize many more analogies than their younger siblings and are thus able to transfer skills and strategies more effectively from one problem to another. The impact of this ability on their success in problem-solving is enormous: the better-informed older child can often solve a problem by analogy, whereas the younger, less well-informed child, unable to see the analogy, must work the solution out from scratch, a much harder task.

Planning How to Solve a Problem

Even the ability to plan how to tackle a problem depends more on the richness of the child's information about the task than on any age-related change in basic planning ability. Traditionally, we thought that young children had only a very limited ability to plan. They certainly weren't very successful in the tasks that measure planning in older children or adults. But new research using situations more suited to infants shows that they can—and do—construct plans and solve problems in both lab tasks and everyday activities. Of course, we cannot be sure exactly how the infant's skills compare with an adult's, since we use very different tasks to measure these skills at different ages. But the evidence suggests that, although younger children may be less successful in planning than their elders, even babies use very much the same planning strategies as everyone else.

Trial and error. The simplest problem-solving plan is to choose a likely way of solving the problem and try it out. If that does not work, you can try another likely course. It is quite obvious that young babies use this kind of strategy—an infant may swing its hands about randomly trying to hit a crib rattle—which is really little more than trial and error. But this simple kind of plan is not unique to babies. Even scientists plan like this in certain circumstances—where, for example, there is nothing else to go on. Edison discovered how to make an effective filament for light bulbs by trying out hundreds of possibilities, one after the other, until he found one that worked, because he did not have enough information about the problem to home in on the solution in a more focused way.

Even when both infant and adult use a trial-and-error

strategy in searching for the solution to a problem, they often go about it in different ways. Two- or three-year-olds will choose successive things to try out in no particular order, while twelve-year-olds will work systematically through a coherent sequence of possibilities. Older children are more likely to be more focused and more sophisticated in the things they try. But these differences are not the direct result of the child's age: in those situations where a child has more experience than an adult, the shoe can be on the other foot (as any parent struggling with their child's latest computer game can testify!).

Analyzing subgoals. A more sophisticated approach to planning is to analyze what needs doing and what order to do it in. For instance, we might imagine two cloths, one with a toy on it, lying on a table. The problem is which cloth to pull to get the toy? Peter Willatts found that babies of nine months can planfully choose which cloth to pull when there are only two cloths, but even at twelve months they get confused if they have to choose among three cloths.[23] By the age of two, however, children have no difficulties with the task.

Children's ability to anticipate and plan continues to expand throughout early childhood. William Fabricius asked children to plan a route to collect baby stuffed animals from buckets and return them to their mothers (see Figure 10).[24] Four-year-olds were not very successful in planning direct routes. They zigzagged backwards and forwards in collecting the baby animals, retracing their steps. By the age of five, however, most children planned more efficient and economical routes. What is interesting about this task is that even the four-year-olds spontaneously corrected their mistakes as they went along, which implies that they are to some extent con-

Forward Search Array

Endpoint-Only Array

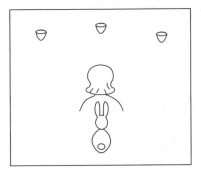

Middle-Only Array

Figure 10

cerned about organizing their problem-solving efficiently. It seems, then, that younger children are only less successful, not less inclined to plan.

Sometimes infants as young as nine months can construct quite elaborate plans, breaking a problem down into subgoals and systematically working through each one. Willatts studied babies trying to get a toy, which was under a cover on the far end of a cloth, which in turn was behind a screen.[25] The baby had to follow a three-step plan—move the screen, pull the cloth, and lift the cover—to get the toy. Very young babies approached this problem in a rather haphazard way, but by the age of nine months, they could often use such a three-step plan successfully.

Of course, the planning involved in Willatts' task is not really very taxing. The infant does not need to choose what to do first because of the way the task is set up. The screen is nearest, and the infant has to move it before it can grasp the cloth. Many problems require a more complicated sort of planning. The child has to choose what order to do things in as well as what to do. This sort of planning is more difficult for young children.

In another study, Willatts changed the problem so that there was a barrier across the cloth. This barrier was out of the baby's reach but could be moved by grasping a handle attached to it and positioned next to the cloth. This task involves two subgoals: removing the barrier and pulling the cloth. Here it is important to get the two actions in the right order. If the child pulls the cloth first, the barrier will dislodge the toy from the cloth, leaving it out of reach. Twelve-month-olds had great difficulty with this task, and only a third of eighteen-month-olds took the barrier away first on even half of their attempts. Two- and three-year-olds normally solve the problem successfully.

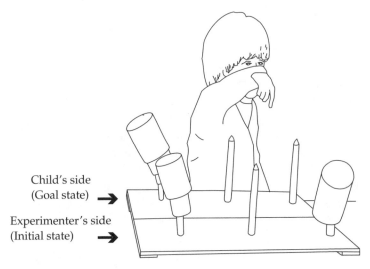

Child's side
(Goal state) ➜

Experimenter's side
(Initial state) ➜

Figure 11

The ability to plan which action to take first develops right through childhood. David Klahr and his colleagues studied this skill using a version of the familiar "Tower of Hanoi" problem (see Figure 11).[26] In the basic version of this task, you have to move a stack of disks from one peg to another, one disk at a time, and never put a larger disk on top of a smaller one. Klahr and Robinson modified the task to make it easier for children to remember the rules: instead of disks, they used "monkey cans" of different sizes—a "daddy" can (biggest), a "mommy" can (middle sized), and a "baby" can (smallest). With these cans, the usual rule is reversed and concretely enforced: a smaller can cannot be put on top of a larger one, since it won't fit. The child did not need to rely on memory to recall what the goal was: there were two complete sets of the puzzle, one showing the solution and the other ready for the child with the cans in the "start" positions. By varying the start position, Klahr and

Robinson could alter the number of steps the child had to plan for to solve the problem.

The emphasis in the Tower of Hanoi problem is on planning the right order in which to make moves and which of the two spare poles to use at each step. With simpler problems, whose solution needed only two steps, 60 to 70 percent of three- and four-year-olds, and all the five- and six-year-olds, were able to plan effectively. Two-thirds of five-year-olds and nearly all the six-year-olds also made perfect plans when this involved looking four moves ahead, although few of the four-year-olds could do this. Over half of the six-year-olds continued to come up with perfect plans when six moves were needed.

What Affects the Child's Ability to Plan?

These developmental changes in planning how to solve problems are puzzling. Some psychologists have suggested that the ability to plan ahead depends on memory capacity.[27] Planning what needs to be done and working out the order in which to do it impose a definite load on memory. These researchers also believe that an individual's memory capacity increases during childhood, which explains why younger children cannot plan as many steps ahead as their elders: their memories are smaller.

The idea of physiological limits on the memory capacity a child brings to the task of planning is quite appealing. Robbie Case has produced some interesting evidence that children's ability to solve problems is indeed related to the memory load imposed by a particular task.[28] The more demanding the task, the older children are likely to be when they can successfully solve it. It is far from clear, however, that this is the whole story. The amount of information a child—or an adult—can hold in mind at one time is not fixed in an absolute way. Most adults can hold around seven unrelated items in mind—

say, seven different things on a shopping list. But if we are able to organize the shopping list and group items together, we can hold many more. For instance, organizing the list into categories (fruits, cleaning materials, dog food) may help us to remember three times as many things as we could if everything were unconnected. The way we understand and organize information affects how much we can hold in mind at any one time.

Memory limits are certainly not the only thing that affects a child's ability to plan. According to Ann Brown and Judy DeLoache, anyone, of any age, can be robbed of the ability to plan effectively if they have insufficient knowledge of the task at hand to allow an adequate recognition of what is and is not relevant.[29] As we saw earlier, even accomplished scientists like Edison cannot always plan effectively. Brown and DeLoache believe that younger children more often plan poorly because of the relatively small amount of knowledge they have so far acquired rather than their age.

To plan effectively, the child needs to know what factors are relevant, what strategies are appropriate or available, and how effective different strategies are. In a task you have not met before, or don't understand very well, it can be very difficult to get a clear picture of these things. There may be no option but to go by trial and error. In such situations, children do not really know what they are doing. Rather than being able to anticipate and plan intelligently for what may come next, they are pretty much at the mercy of events. A slightly more sophisticated knowledge of the task may overcome some of these problems and allow the child to begin planning in a systematic way. But partial understanding of a task can produce variable results, as we saw in the case of Siegler's balance task: the five-year-olds know enough to answer systematically but not enough to understand why some of their answers are systematically wrong. Not understanding the limitations of a strategy can reduce the payoffs from planning ahead. If taking the trouble to work out the answer is (apparently) only randomly successful, then why waste the effort? Guessing may be just as good. Factors like this may explain why young children will plan in simple situations but act impulsively without planning in more complex ones. Where the cost of planning is slight, or the payoff certain, it may be worth trying to plan rigorously, but the payoffs may not be big enough to encourage the young child to plan in complex or poorly understood situations. Knowing the limitations of your knowledge and solution strategies, on the other hand (as the fourteen-year-olds do in Siegler's balance scale task), can allow you to choose more selectively and more accurately when to use what you know in planning and when it is just as well to guess.

Brown and DeLoache's account of children's problems with planning fits very well with Annette Karmiloff-Smith's theory of what it is that changes as children's problem-solving becomes more sophisticated and more successful.[30] Studying a wide range of problem-solving tasks, Karmiloff-Smith has identified three major phases through which the child passes on the way to competent mastery of a given aspect of a problem: the data-driven phase, the theory-driven phase, and the metatheory-driven phase. Phases are not like stages of development: a child can simultaneously be in the data-driven phase in one task and in the metatheory-driven phase in another. Which phase a child has reached in a particular task is a matter of the child's degree of knowledge and experience with that specific task domain.

The first phase is the position of a novice. When we first tackle a new problem, our knowledge is fragmentary and disconnected. We do not know how one thing relates to another, and we are not in a good position to make predictions or understand what happens as we try to solve the problem. At this state of knowledge, we tend to take a trial-and-error approach, and to let those aspects of the task we can use for feedback drive our actions. An individual at this state of knowledge is necessarily "data-driven," but "data-driven" actions can become very efficient and successful.

As we learn more and make new discoveries, things become a little more organized, and we can discern a clearer structure. At this second phase, we can begin to put things together, try to figure out how one thing connects to another, and develop theories that allow us to make predictions. Having a theory means that we can approach problems in a more planful fashion.[31] We can become "theory-driven" problem-solvers.

Trying to solve problems with no guiding theory can be very ineffective. A child may notice that one thing is successful and another is not but have no basis for understanding why, or for planning the next move. But acting solely in terms of a theory can be just as damaging: an incorrect or inadequate theory can blind us to information the theory does not cover and prevent us from using feedback that does not fit the theory or from making new discoveries.[32] Ideal problem-solving would not only be theory driven, it would also involve theories structured to allow even unexpected input from the task to be examined and explored. This last is the essence of a mature approach to monitoring the success of one's reasoning and regulating it in an intelligent and planful way. It requires more sophisticated knowledge than a theory-based approach, but it also demands an explicit recognition that one's theory is *only* a theory. This sort of sophistication is the third, or metatheory phase.

Karmiloff-Smith has shown that the sequence of data-driven, theory-driven, and metatheory-driven phases she has identified occurs in many different types of problem-solving as children develop into more sophisticated problem-solvers in each domain. The whole three-phase cycle can occur over and over in a particular task as the child's first triumph over some aspect of the task uncovers a new aspect of the problem.

In sum, work like that of Brown, DeLoache, and Karmiloff-Smith explains why it is that children have difficulty in planning their problem-solving and why this difficulty gradually declines. Each step forward in planning depends on a step forward in what you know about the specifics of the task. You cannot effectively monitor the progress of a method of solution if you do not have a coherent method in mind or if you are overloaded with apparently disconnected bits of information. You cannot planfully decide between several alternative courses of action if you do not know that different options exist or if you do not know the relative advantages and disadvantages of each alternative. You cannot reflect on the relationship between different courses of action if you cannot represent those actions in a useful way. Thus increases in specific knowledge of the task are essential for the development of the more abstract and reflective metacognitive knowledge that allows us to monitor and regulate problem-solving successfully.

The Child as a Novice Problem-Solver

The research I have discussed in this chapter shows that the development of problem-solving is, in many ways, just the opposite of what we have traditionally believed. Problem-solving has its roots in innately specified skills, rather than in specifically logical constructions. The development of problem-solving depends on an increase in factual information to a far greater extent than we previously supposed. Skill develops in fragments, since knowledge in each domain grows at its own pace, rather than passing through general stages encompassing all types of problems. Although general processes do play a role in problem-solving, they are more dependent on, and more intertwined with, factual knowledge than we used to think. What the child knows about a problem domain is a critical factor in how he or she addresses that problem. Changes in what an individual typically knows in infancy, childhood, and adolescence play a vital role in creating the developmental changes we see in problem-solving.

The important role played by information and understanding in the development of problem-solving skill is underlined by studies comparing expert adult problem-solvers with novices. Being an expert problem-solver in one area does not mean that you will be an expert at solving all types of problems. Typically, experts in solving problems in one area (such as chess or science) are quite poor at solving other kinds of problems (like fixing the plumbing or composing an opera)—and vice versa. Equally, expertise in solving a particular type of problem does not depend on higher than average general intelligence. What experts have over novices is not more general ability, but rather, a better informed and richer way of looking at problems in their particular area of expertise, one that is based on their more varied and extensive experience.

Adrian De Groot's studies of chess players offer a good illustration of expertise.[33] Experts at chess have learned to recognize patterns that are simply invisible to a novice. Where the novice worries about thirty-two separate *pieces*, the expert may be thinking about just three *patterns*. Chess problems look a lot simpler to the expert than they do to the novice. In addition, the expert will have experience of many games of chess, and so will be able to anticipate how the game will develop, which the novice cannot. By remembering past games, the expert may be able to recall good strategies for particular problems, while the novice will have to work out what to do from scratch—a much more difficult task. Knowledge and experience, rather than general ability or special intelligence, create expertise and simplify problem-solving. This is just as true of child chess experts as of adult ones—Michelene Chi has shown that chess expertise depends less on age than on rich representations of the problem.[34]

There is a sense in which the young child is a "universal novice" in comparison with older children or adults. Inevitably, young children have had less experience than their elders in most areas because they have had less time to make the discoveries or to identify the information that is common to an adolescent or adult. As we have seen, the richer representations of a topic that come from greater information and experience can fundamentally change the individual's concepts in that area and the inference he or she can draw. They can even reduce the extent to which the individual must work at identifying the nature of the problem and the best strategy to use in solving it. Small wonder that young children's problem-solving is usually so much less sophisticated and successful than that of their elders!

4 / Working through a Problem and Discovering New Strategies

Success in solving problems depends on the kinds of inferences children are able to draw, the aspects of the task they recognize and understand, and the strategies they bring to the problem. As we saw in the last chapter, these things change throughout childhood as children gain experience and knowledge about the problem at hand. Yet, while this goes some way toward explaining why a child may succeed—or not succeed—in solving a given problem, it does not tell the whole story. Problem-solving is a dynamic activity that draws on processes for bringing skills and knowledge to bear in particular situations.

The Dynamics of Solving Problems

This chapter will look at the processes that shape children's problem-solving as they actually interact with the task. The same dynamic processes are involved whether the problem-solver is two or twenty years old, even if the results produced by those processes at different ages—or by different individuals—are sometimes quite different.

What are the key problem-solving processes? Let's go back to the example at the beginning of Chapter 1: Simon and James, wrestling with the problems of building a shelter from the odds and ends lying around the yard. Games like this often start with a clear idea of the goal— a shelter "just like Robinson Crusoe's in the film," or a fortress, or some such. As the children engage the task, their idea of what the final shelter should be like almost always shifts, becoming less ambitious in some ways and more ambitious in others. The realities of the situation (the obvious absence of a natural cave in the backyard, Mother's objections to their cannibalizing the toolshed for materials, and the like) often constrain children's idea of what they are trying to do. At the same time, the idea of the final goal continues to grow and change right through the game as new discoveries create new options: finding a broomstick may suggest a flagpole, for example; burlap sacking could become curtains or a hammock.

Almost all problem-solving involves this constant updating and modifying of goals. Some problems seem to have a very specific, clearly defined goal ($2 + 5 = ?$, for example). But even here, there may be subgoals to be decided on (such as whether to go for accuracy by working out the right answer or for speed by guessing at it, and so on). An important part of solving a problem is discerning what the goals are, and a key element in that process is the interaction between the child and the problem, and the feedback that comes from addressing the problem in different ways.

Along with changes in goals, children's strategies evolve as they interact with the task. In my example, the two children began by trying to balance branches of bracken on top of the shelter to make a roof, heaping them by armfuls any old way. By the end of the afternoon, they had abandoned this approach and were working systematically across the roof interweaving each individual bracken branch with the others. Simon and James discovered from experience that heaped up bracken falls off, while woven bracken stays where they want it, and they changed their approach accordingly.

This process of learning from interacting with the task is one of the key aspects of problem-solving. How do children do it? What sort of feedback do they use? How do they figure out what is wrong when their strategy does not work out?

The example of the two boys building their shelter also illustrates another crucial aspect of problem-solving, one that we often tend to neglect. As they worked on the shelter, the boys encountered problems they had never met before: how to move a gatepost far too heavy for a grown man to lift; what to substitute for ropes to tie things together. Solving novel problems like these calls for an act of creativity, an inventive move that will take the child to a strategy or an idea that is entirely new—at least to that individual. Not all problems call for such acts of creativity; some can be solved by carefully choosing the order in which to proceed (like the Tower of Hanoi) or which of several possibilities to pursue (as in the arithmetic problem above). But many problems require creative thinking.

Children are astonishingly resourceful in coming up with new strategies and solutions as they solve problems. How do they do it? How, in my example, did Simon and James hit upon the idea of sliding their gatepost across rollers, or using thatching instead of rope? Feedback from a task can tell children they are doing the wrong thing, but how do they then go on to discover, or invent, a better approach?

The key processes in solving problems—choosing between strategies, responding to feedback, and inventing new strategies—have something important in common.

They are about *change*—from initial to later strategies and from known to new strategies. Change is the essence of problem-solving.

Selecting for Success

Researchers such as Robert Siegler and his associates have emphasized that children almost always have more than one potential strategy to use in solving a problem.[1] A baby trying to put a square peg in a round hole can bang the peg up and down harder and harder, or twist it about, or try a new hole—or simply throw the aggravating object away. If we watch children trying to solve problems, we will often see a succession of different strategies being used in quite a short period of time— two or three, say, over a span of five minutes. How does the child choose which strategy to start with and which to use next? And how over a longer period—sometimes within an hour, sometimes over a number of years—does the strategy first chosen come to change?

The details of any problem normally offer a number of cues that match up with situations a child has encountered before. Various courses of action come to mind (such as banging the peg harder or twisting it in the "square peg" problem), and each of these strategies has a sort of "history" in the child's experience. That is to say, each strategy has been used successfully or unsuccessfully in various situations. The more successful a strategy has been in a particular situation, the more likely it is that the child will choose it again in that situation, as well as in other, seemingly similar tasks. Siegler found that children choose the strategy most associated with success, so if a particular child has been very successful in solving other "putting-blocks-into-things" problems by using a "brute force" strategy, something like banging the peg harder and harder will also be the first strategy the child chooses in the square peg–round hole problem.

Siegler's account of how a child chooses the initial approach to a problem also explains how that child goes on to choose other strategies, and in time comes to prefer a more appropriate strategy as a first choice.[2] Each encounter with the task adds to the "history" of the strategy the child tries out. If the child solves the problem, the association between that strategy and success is strengthened, and the child becomes even more likely to use that strategy for that type of problem. But if the child does not solve the problem, the association of that strategy with success weakens. Eventually, it may fall below some threshold, to be replaced by a different strategy more highly associated with success than the original one. This alternative strategy is then chosen for the task, and is likely to become the child's first choice in encounters with new problems of a similar kind.[3]

Siegler's account also explains why children's approach to problem-solving can sometimes be inconsistent, using a variety of strategies and seeming not to prefer one over another. When a child is new to a problem, he or she may have no one strategy that is definitively associated with success. Instead, there may be two or three possibilities, each with a relatively limited history, a low association with success in that type of task, and little to choose from between them. For example, a baby who is new to the problem of putting varying shapes into different-sized holes may have been as unsuccessful in trying a different hole (because she has not happened to find the right one) as in whacking the peg or twisting it around. There is no clear basis for choosing among these three strategies, so which one the child chooses will reflect idiosyncrasies in the child or in the problem, and will vary from one attempt to another.

Siegler has found that there is a threshold below which children do not seem to discriminate between strategies.[4] So long as different strategies are all within a certain range in terms of their association with success, a child is no more likely to select one strategy than another. Only when one strategy becomes sufficiently more associated with success than its competitors does the child systematically choose that strategy. And different children set this "threshold of distinctiveness" differently. One child, for example, might begin to try different holes in the "square peg" problem systematically as soon as that strategy is, say, 20 percent more associated with success than any other. Another child might continue to sample all the possible strategies until trying a new hole is 80 percent more associated with success than its rivals. It is not yet clear what accounts for this difference between one child and another, but its implications for how fast and even what different children can learn are quite obvious.

Siegler's work also explains why, after having discovered it, a child might not immediately start to use the best strategy for a given problem. The strategy of trying a different hole in the "square peg" problem has no "history" for a child who is using it for the first time. Even though it is successful, the association with success may still be smaller than that built up for other strategies in similar tasks, such as the brute force strategy. Until the new strategy has had a chance to cross the threshold of distinctiveness, it is not likely to be systematically chosen.

That a strategy's association with success is both the vital factor determining which strategy a child chooses in first approaching a problem and the key to changes in strategy during problem-solving is really an old idea in a new context. The basic mechanism for change is competition between different responses until one becomes more clearly associated with success than another. Learning through selective competition between responses is a universal mechanism for development and change. Processes of this sort were studied by animal psychologists in the first part of this century, and are the basis on which much of animal behavior is explained. The process of selecting things because they are successful is also the mechanism through which evolution works: successful individuals (or strategies) survive and go on to breed (or be used again), whereas unsuccessful ones die out (or are not used) and become extinct.

Some researchers believe that the process of selecting for success can wholly explain the dynamic processes of change in problem-solving. David Klahr and his associates have written computer programs to simulate how children learn to solve problems (like the balance scale described in Chapter 3) using the competitive selection principle as the key to the process of developing more successful strategies.[5] These computer simulations are quite impressive: they often behave very much as real children do in tackling the same problems. They provide strong evidence of the problem-solving power of the process of selection for success.

This approach, however, does not explain all the effects we see in children's problem-solving. For example, "selection for success" focuses on how skill develops from efforts to avoid failure. A great deal of the change that we see in a child's approach to solving a problem is produced in just this way. But if selection for success were the *only* process of change in problem-solving, we would not expect children to move away from successful strategies once they had adopted one consistently—there should be no reason to make such a change—yet children *do* move away from consistently successful strategies. Obviously, changes in problem-solving must also result from other processes. Furthermore, the process of selecting for success can explain how a child comes to choose which of several known strategies to use and how these strategies might get refined and improved. But it does not explain how a child might discover a new, qualitatively different strategy that is not already in his or her repertoire. Only strategies the child has already used can acquire a "history," or be compared to other strategies. So where do entirely new strategies come from?

Learning from Success

Problem-solving involves the process of trying out strategies in the search for a solution and dropping the unsuccessful ones. But surprisingly often, children who have already discovered a successful strategy will alter and improve it in ways that cannot be directly explained as responses to feedback about success or failure.

In the course of her research, Annette Karmiloff-Smith has described many examples of children who alter already successful strategies as they tackle problems.[6] For example, children of seven to twelve years were asked to make a map so that they could drive a toy ambulance from a house to the hospital on a "road" drawn on a long roll of paper. The child first drove the ambulance on a practice run "without the patient" to discover the route. The route had many T junctions, where one turning led to a cul-de-sac and the other to the hospital. Some of these had landmarks, such as trees or zigzags, but others did not. The paper was always partly rolled up (see Figure 12), so that the child could not look ahead and see which turning was the right one in advance. The

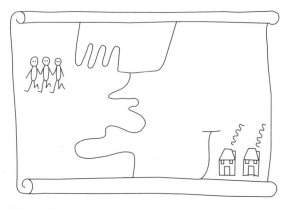

Figure 12

child's problem was to find a way of recording the route accurately, so that the ambulance could drive directly to its destination on the real run "with the patient."

The children in Karmiloff-Smith's study had no difficulty in devising ways of making maps of this route, and they used many different styles. Some children drew complete maps of the whole route in miniature. Others drew each individual turning, ignoring the straight road in between, and used marks, arrows, or colors to show which way to turn. Still others used the landmarks, creating descriptions such as "turn toward the trees . . . then take the zigzag side" and so on. Some children simply noted the direction of the turning: "turn left . . . right . . . left . . . left."

Some of the styles children adopted for recording the route could not accommodate every turning, and the children tended to modify these strategies as they went along, as we would expect. A child who was recording landmarks such as trees or zigzags, for example, would run into problems on those turnings that had no landmarks. But other styles would allow a successful map to be made of the whole route. Any system for recording whether the turning was to the left or to the right would work, whether it depicted the information in words or as a drawing (see Figure 13a). What is most interesting about Karmiloff-Smith's results is that children often altered these *successful* strategies too, sometimes introducing new detail into the drawing (see Figure 13b). Effects of this sort are not driven by feedback from the task or selection for success in any obvious way.

Changes in successful strategies of the kind described by Karmiloff-Smith show that, like associations with success, conceptual understanding also plays a role in the evolution of problem-solving strategies. Karmiloff-Smith believes that the changes children make in successful

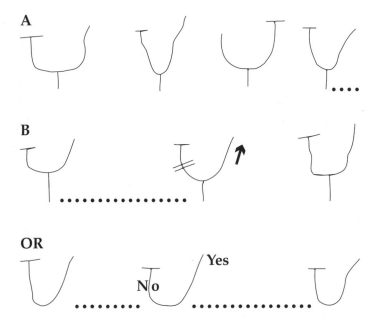

Figure 13

strategies reveal the activity of processes that are always striving to make more sense of things.[7] Having a strategy that will solve the problem creates a space for reflecting on that strategy and finding other ways to represent what is going on more explicitly—and perhaps discovering things that were only implicit before but which can now be more explicitly represented. These discoveries can then feed back to embellish or improve the strategy in ways that reflect not simply the literal requirements of the task in hand but the child's growing understanding.

This conceptual process for change in problem-solving is not in conflict with the feedback-driven process of selecting for success described by Siegler. Rather, it is an extra layer of processing that builds on the successful strategies selection for success provides. It need not be a conscious or deliberate process: children may be quite unaware of exactly why they have altered a successful strategy.

Shifting between Similar Strategies

This process—making new discoveries by reflecting on the elements implicit in a successful strategy—begins to explain where new strategies come from. Many quite striking changes in children's problem-solving may come about in just this way. Certainly, there are a great many instances in which a new strategy is clearly related to an old one, the new strategy taking more efficient advantage of elements that were only implicit in the old. Robert Siegler and Eric Jenkins's study of children learning to add up small numbers provides one such example.[8]

Five- to seven-year-old children may know as many as four different strategies for adding small numbers, such as $5 + 3$, together:

Remembering: they can try to remember what the answer was last time.

Counting everything out: they can count out each of the numbers on their fingers—one, two, three, four, five on the left hand, for example, and one, two, three on the right—and then count all the raised fingers across both hands: one, two, three, four, five, six, seven, eight.

Counting on from the larger number: they can take the larger number for granted and count out only the smaller one on their fingers, starting from five: five, six, seven, eight.

Decomposing: with more difficult sums, such as 12 + 3, children of this age may decompose the sum into easier elements, such as $12 + 3 = 10 + (2 + 3)$.

Five- to seven-year-olds tend to vary which of these strategies they use, depending on the details of the problem. With some sums, a child may be confident that remembering the answer will work out, but with other types of sums, retrieving the answer from memory may not have been much associated with success in the past, and so the child chooses another strategy. Children select the strategy that is most likely to work successfully for each individual problem.

Younger children do not know many strategies for adding numbers together; few four-year-olds know about counting on from the larger number, for instance. But by testing children regularly over a number of weeks, Siegler and Jenkins were able to follow how some of these children discovered it. At first, the majority of them added numbers together by counting everything out, one number on each hand, and then recounting across all the fingers. Discovering the "counting on" strategy involved

1, 2, 3, 4, 5,   ...1, 2, 3,   1, 2, 3, 4, 5,   6, 7, 8

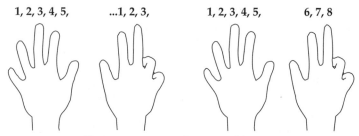

First strategy: counting everything out.

1, 2, 3, 4, 5,   ...6, 7, 8

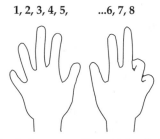

Intermediate strategy: counting out the first number and
then counting on.

5, ...6, 7, 8

Final strategy: counting on from the first number.

Figure 14

a separate, intermediary step, as Figure 14 shows. Having counted out the first of the numbers to be added on the left hand, as in the original strategy, the child continues, counting the second number on from the first (saying "six, seven, eight") without explicitly counting out those three fingers first. This strategy is only a slight modification of the original "count everything out" strategy, but it leads the way to a further step: *not* counting out the first figure before starting the addition. The child has discovered the "counting on" strategy through a sequence of small steps that build on elements implicit in the original strategy.

Discovering Something Different

Not all new strategies seem so continuous with the old as those in Siegler's study of children mastering addition. Often in problem-solving, a child needs to abandon the original approach completely and search for an entirely new type of strategy, rather than simply drawing forth the implicit elements of the old one. A child building a bridge with wooden blocks might begin by using a strategy that focuses on finding spans of sufficient length to rest across simple supports. But if the gap to be bridged is longer than the longest block, the child will have to switch from attending to length and focus on the entirely different problem of constructing counterbalance supports for two shorter spans.

When there is a qualitative strategy change of this kind, it can be hard to see how the new strategy relates to the old—and even where the new strategy came from. Yet detailed studies of children's problem-solving are beginning to show us how qualitative changes in strategy come about. In fact, it is often possible to trace a continuous thread between an old and a new strategy, even where the two strategies are very different in character. The initial strategy a child uses to tackle a problem makes some aspects of the problem seem very salient or relevant and others less so. The child attends to the salient factors and, in the course of working out the goals and subgoals suggested by the seemingly salient factors, discovers aspects of the task that were not apparent before. These discoveries arise directly out of feedback from the original strategy. New discoveries lead to shifts in which factors the child sees as relevant to the problem, and so to shifts in what the child attends to. As the child's attention moves to these new factors, his or her behavior and interaction with the task change. This in turn brings the child new kinds of feedback from the task, making it possible to go on to still further discoveries, and so on. No one new discovery need be very big: a succession of quite small discoveries gradually creates a continuous stream of steps, each a little different from, but overlapping with, what went before, gradually easing the child from one strategy to another, very different one.

This process is illustrated by an example from a study I did of children building bridges with wooden blocks.[9] The children in this experiment were given a tub of blocks of different shapes and sizes. A mat on the floor had a river painted across it, and banks painted on either side. The problem was to build a bridge across the river, so that "people could get across safely." It would not be possible to put any blocks in the river, because "it is a very dangerous river, very deep, with very fast water." None of the blocks was long enough to form a single span from one side to the other.

Most five-year-old children have a great deal of difficulty with this problem, and many cannot solve it at all. But some do successfully discover what needs doing. Lucy, aged five, began the task by trying to build a

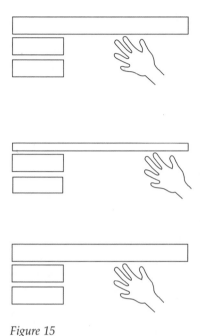

Figure 15

simple support bridge. Her plan was to find a block long enough to span the river and to rest it across two supports, one on either side of the river. She spent some time looking for the longest blocks and measuring different blocks up against the river. She tried long thin blocks and long fat blocks (see Figure 15), and then she tried the same blocks again. After eleven separate attempts to solve the problem this way (and breaking off to accuse the experimenter of not having brought the right blocks!), she finally concluded that none of the blocks was long enough to span the river.

At this point, Lucy's basic strategy suggests a new subgoal: if no one block is long enough to cross the river by itself, make a longer span by using two. In this second phase of problem-solving, Lucy quickly found two blocks

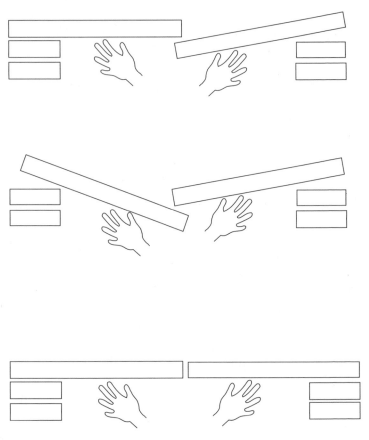

Figure 16

that together could stretch across the river. The problem of length was solved! But how could the two spans be fastened together? She tried them in various relationships: abutting, end on, with the left-hand block overlapping the right-hand one, and vice versa (see Figure 16). Her new goal became finding a way of fastening the blocks together. After trying various possible ways the two spans might meet mid river for a while—sometimes pressing the blocks together in position as if to make them stick—Lucy did something rather surprising (though it is something Piaget observed in a similar task): she put a small block between the two spans at the point where they met in mid river and squeezed the whole arrangement together tightly (Figure 17). The small block was apparently intended to act as a "fastener" to stop the two spans from falling apart. Obviously, the plan did not work. Lucy quickly recognized that the "fastener" had not improved the situation and removed it.

Up to this point, Lucy had not paid much attention to the towers she had built on either side of the river. She had put them in place at the very beginning and then left them alone. Nor had she tried to secure the spans to the towers, or even to rest the spans on the towers unsupported. She never let go of the blocks she was trying out. She either held them in place by gripping along the length of each block or by pressing very firmly down on the tower end (see Figures 15 and 16).

It happened that, when Lucy attempted to fasten the two spans together with the small block (Figure 17), she tried to support the structure by pressing down over one tower (gently, and hopefully, letting go to see if the bridge would work). When this effort failed, she went back to holding the two spans in place by pressing heav-

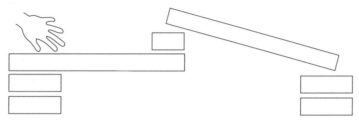

Figure 17

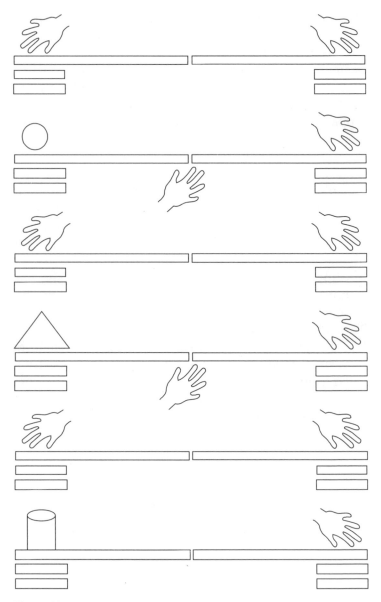

Figure 18

ily on each span above the towers. Did this last experience suggest to her the idea of fastening the spans to the towers, rather than fastening them together? It seems likely that it did, for Lucy now began to work on how to fasten the spans down to the towers.

During this third phase of problem-solving, Lucy tried out a variety of blocks as "fasteners," placing each one in turn on top of the span, where it rested on the tower. In effect, the small block replaced her hand as a fastener. A striking thing about this phase is that Lucy clearly had no understanding of how a block might help fasten a span in place: all the blocks she tried out were far too light to counterbalance the weight of the span. She systematically chose small, light blocks and did not try to manipulate the weight of the "fastener" at all (Figure 18). From this and other errors it is plain that Lucy conceptualized these blocks as fastenings, or as surrogate hands, rather than as weights. None of her efforts were at all successful, and she alternated between trying to fasten the spans to the towers and reverting fruitlessly to her original plan of finding one block long enough to span the river by itself (Figure 19).

Although Lucy was not very successful in fastening the spans to the towers in this third phase, the fact that she adopted this plan was a significant step in her problem-solving process. For the first time, she had begun to put blocks in the right position to act as counterweights for the spans, even though she herself did not yet understand, or intend to use, counterweights. Because she has put the blocks in the right place, Lucy will now get feedback that is relevant to the idea of counterbalance, even though she *thinks* she is looking for a fastener. As she proceeds, she will discover that heavier "fasteners" are more successful than lighter ones, and this feedback will then be available for her to explore. Lucy's interac-

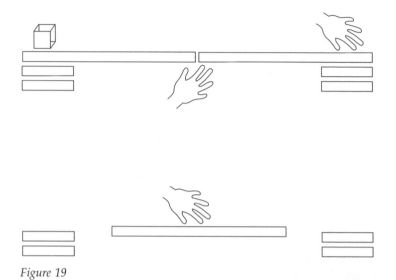

Figure 19

tion with the task generated by her goal of *fastening* can potentially lead her to pay attention to weight, and thus to a counterbalance solution.

This is just what happened. Eventually, Lucy noticed that bigger blocks worked better as fasteners than smaller ones: the bridge still fell in at the middle, but the effort needed to hold the spans in place was greater when the fastener was smaller. Lucy began systematically to choose bigger blocks to try as fasteners. She noticed that bigger blocks were heavier and began to try more than one block on each end of the bridge (Figure 20 top) to increase the weight. But the more blocks she balanced up as fasteners, the more unstable the towers became. Lucy then moved on to a new goal: devising more stable towers to support a big enough weight to fasten the span in place (Figure 20 bottom).

In this fourth phase of problem-solving, Lucy was directly attending to the principal factors relevant to building a counterbalance bridge: the amount and position of the weight and the problems of balance. She was finally able to build a successful, stable counterbalance bridge and thus solved the problem (Figure 21). It is not at all clear that Lucy herself fully understood the principles underlying her strategy, or that she would have been able to describe or explain them at all well. Quite likely, the key principles remained implicit in her strategy, rather than being explicitly articulated. Nonetheless, Lucy's strategy exposed her to all the right feedback to allow her to go on and discover the principles of counterbalance in an explicit way.

This example clearly shows how a succession of tiny steps, each arising from the child's current problem-solving, can gradually lead to major changes in strategy and understanding. The evolution of goals and subgoals stemming from the old strategy can inspire new, radically different strategies. Two important points emerge from

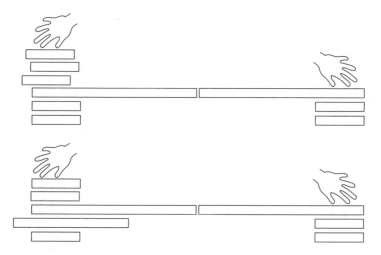

Figure 20

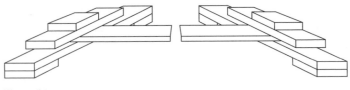

Figure 21

in-depth studies of processes like these. First, the development of new, qualitatively different strategies is an interactive process that relies on feedback from the task rather than on processes entirely internal to the child. Second, what feedback a child notices is itself determined by the strategy the child is using. Some strategies direct the child toward factors relevant to the solution, while others do not.

The role of a particular strategy in directing a child's attention is clearly illustrated in Lucy's efforts: as long as her plan was to find the longest block, she did not notice the relevance of weight. At each decision point in her problem-solving, Lucy and the other five-year-olds who were successful in solving the "bridge" problem made choices that led them toward new subgoals, which were effective in directing them to the right factors. Other children took other routes and were not successful. Almost all five-year-olds begin this task by looking for the longest block. Some never give up on this; instead of moving on to the goal of trying to make a longer block out of two, they simply widen their search for the "missing" block that will be long enough. Their strategy is reasonable, but it directs them away from the factors relevant to solving the problem. Not all five-year-olds who do decide to build a longer block go on to the instructive subgoal of "fastening" things together (though virtually all who completed the task did do just that). Some children become fixated on the idea of a third (illegal) tower in the middle of the river to support the free ends of the two spans. But again, this strategy diverts them from the factors relevant to counterbalance, and none of the children who adopted it solved the problem successfully. Some children tried to make cardboard barges to support the central tower, or to build dams further up the river to overcome the "danger" that prohibited this approach. Others were diverted into more esoteric and surreal realms. Jack (aged five) began to build a third tower in the middle of the river to support the two spans he had chosen. The experimenter said, "Oh-oh! *Whoosh!* It's a very dangerous river, look, the water runs so fast, it rushes the blocks away . . ." After a pause, the child countered with, "Well, the strongest man in all the world comes along, and he builds the tower!" And after the "strongest man" had also been "whooshed away" the child said, "He swims back, and he *drinks all the water!* Then he builds the tower anyway."

Strategy-Driven Change

The particular strategy children use can determine what discoveries they can make and thus what new strategies they can invent or explore, even in situations where they may already be solving the problem successfully.

Take, for example, the Twenty Questions game. In this parlor game, one player secretly chooses an object (when children play, the choice is usually made from a tray of objects). The other player(s) must find out what the secret object is by asking questions that can only be answered by "yes" or "no."

Playing with the sixteen variously colored objects shown in Figure 22, children five to ten years old can solve the problem successfully, but they use a range of different strategies. Older children tend to try to narrow down the

Figure 22

search by asking about a whole group of objects with a single question: "Is it a car?" In this way they eliminate all the cars if the answer to the question is "No!" Almost all nine-year-olds use this strategy, while less than 50 percent of seven-year-olds and 40 percent of five-year-olds approach the problem in this way. Instead, these younger children ask about each object individually, identifying it in one of several different ways. It is often quite difficult to get children to switch from asking about individual objects to asking about groups of objects before the age of about eight. What I have found most interesting about the results of this task is that perhaps 20 percent of children at both five and seven years will spontaneously switch to asking about groups of objects during the course of playing a few games of Twenty Questions. What is even more interesting, making this switch is associated with certain strategies for identifying individual objects but not with others.

In a study I carried out, children used four different strategies for identifying individual objects:

1. *Touching:* touching a particular object and saying no more than "That one?"
2. *Naming:* indicating an object by touching or pointing and saying the object's name ("the car?").
3. *Adjective:* indicating an object by touching or pointing and mentioning some property of the object ("the red one?").
4. *Full description:* providing a unique description of the object ("the red car?").

Children using the "touching" strategy and the "full description" strategy seldom made any change in their approach, and none of these children ever switched to asking about a group of objects. But every child who began the experiment using the "naming" or "adjective" strategies moved to another strategy at some point during the game, and over half of the children of both ages who used these two strategies switched to asking about a group of objects. Table 1 shows the strength of the relationship between the child's initial strategy and the

Table 1   Changes in strategy as a function of the child's initial
strategy

Initial strategy	Children changing to any other strategy (%)	Children changing from asking about individual objects to asking about groups (%)
Touch	10	0
Name	100	55
Adjective	100	50
Description	17	0

likelihood of making this change to a qualitatively different approach.

This kind of effect is intriguing. The children were not told to play quickly or to ask as few questions as possible; they were under no *external* pressure to improve or change their approach, and all the strategies for identifying individual objects were successful in solving the problem. Nor was there any objective difficulty attached to any of the strategies. The "naming" and the "adjective" strategies *seem* to present a problem, in that each provides only a partial, and therefore a potentially ambiguous verbal identification (which car or red one does the child mean?), but in fact, there was no ambiguity: children using these strategies clarified their question by touching or pointing out the object they meant.

Nonetheless, the *potential* for ambiguity inherent in the "naming" and the "adjective" strategies was the key factor triggering the children's switch to questions about groups of objects. These strategies direct the child's attention to the *possibility* that ambiguity might arise from the presence of more than one car or more than one red thing. These two strategies thus make the presence of a group of similar objects salient, while the "touching" and "full description" strategies do not. By noticing that there are groups of things and that the answer to a given question *might apply equally to all members of a group,* the child begins to look in the right direction to discover or invent the strategy of asking directly about a group of objects.

There is nothing inherent in the "naming" or the "adjective" strategies that makes them draw the child toward asking about groups of objects. The effect comes from the *interaction* of these strategies with the task at hand. If the objects used are changed, so that there is no potential ambiguity to be made salient by the "naming" or the "adjective" strategy, these two strategies are no more associated with switching to questions about groups of objects than are the "touching" and "full description" strategies.

Each object in Figure 23, for example, can be uniquely identified by a basic category name of the kind Eleanor Rosch has shown five-year-olds prefer ("car," for example, rather than "vehicle").[10] Playing with these objects, five-year-olds who identify single objects by name are no more likely than those using touch to switch to asking about groups of objects—or to make any other change in their strategy. In fact, with these materials, few children made any sort of change in their strategy, and none switched from asking about individual objects to asking about groups, a marked contrast to the results we see when children play with the objects shown in Figure 22. This cannot be explained by saying that the children playing with the objects in Figure 23 did not happen to think of the idea of asking about groups of objects, or that they could not see groupings of these objects. Half of the children in this study had just played Twenty Questions with the objects in Figure 22 and had been chosen for the second task because they had spontane-

Figure 23

Table 2 Changes in strategy as a function of the child's initial strategy, for five-year-olds using the objects shown in Figure 22 and Figure 23

Initial strategy	Children changing to any other strategy (%)		Children changing from asking about individual objects to asking about groups (%)	
	Figure 22	Figure 23	Figure 22	Figure 23
Touch	17	42	0	0
Name	100	0	50	0
Adjective	N.A.	N.A.	N.A.	N.A.
Description	0	N.A.	0	N.A.

ously asked about groups of objects in that first game. In addition, all the children sorted the objects into categories (vehicle, fruit, furniture, clothing) spontaneously when asked to put like things together after the game. The strikingly different results produced by the two collections of objects (summarized in Table 2) show that the strategy of identifying the objects by name only induces change when the detailed context of the task makes names potentially ambiguous.

Do Problem-Solving Processes Develop?

The dynamic processes of ongoing problem-solving—selection for success, reflecting on and making explicit what was only implicit in previous strategies, and the processes that generate new strategies through the interaction between goals and feedback—do not change during the course of childhood. These processes operate in the same way from birth to adulthood. Indeed, babies could not develop if this were not so: the dynamic processes of problem-solving are essential tools for conceptual development as a whole. They provide the means by which the child's abilities grow.

Of course, the fact that infants and adolescents have the same dynamic processes for problem-solving does not mean that a two-year-old and a fifteen-year-old will make the same discoveries in a given task or be equally capable of solving it. Differences in knowledge and experience generally mean that younger and older individuals adopt quite different strategies when they first address a problem. Different strategies mean different discoveries and different probabilities of success, as we have seen. Young children are less successful in solving problems than their elders not because they are any less adept at the dynamics of problem-solving but because they are more likely to start out with weaker strategies.

5 / The Social Context of Children's Problem-Solving

Infants and children have an immense curiosity about the world and a determined drive to understand the things going on around them. In a profound sense, young children are the authors and architects of their own problem-solving skills: actively engaging the world; exploring and making discoveries; interpreting, structuring, and organizing information about tasks and about the effects of differing courses of action, all the while building up the experience on which problem-solving expertise is based.

Nonetheless, the child's own resources are not enough to achieve skilled, mature problem-solving. In some cases, it is quite obvious that an individual child working alone is unlikely to discover the requisite knowledge and skills. There are many things, such as the population of New Zealand, the date of Neil Armstrong's moon walk, the nature of electricity, the cross-product rule for solving balance scale tasks, how to bake meringues, and so on, that children cannot be expected to discover firsthand, even from hints and clues. These things must be passed on by other people.

Even in situations that seem to rely only on our perceptions of the physical world, social factors often play a critical role. Take, for instance, Piaget's famous conservation task: the child is shown two beakers of different shapes, one of which contains some water. The water is poured from one beaker to the other, and the child must say whether the amount of water is still the same, even though it now reaches a different height on the beaker. The correct answer to the problem is usually taken to be that there is still the same amount of water.

But this is not strictly true, in fact, as Paul Light and Anne-Nelly Perret-Clermont have pointed out.[1] The first beaker will still be damp inside when the water is poured out of it. Some water must therefore be left behind, so the answer that the amount in the second beaker is "the same" is, strictly speaking, wrong. It is the right answer only in light of the shared definitions of what is or is not relevant to the task at hand.[2] A key part of becoming a mature problem-solver is learning the shared assumptions and meanings of our culture—learning what is regarded as a good solution to a problem and what is not.

In fact, sharing the task of solving a problem turns out to be one of the key processes through which children learn the skills they need to become mature problem-solvers. Children learn a lot from watching other people, from listening, and even from simply solving problems in a social setting.[3] They love to do things with other people—to join in with the chores and help out, to play games or tackle puzzles sociably. Joining in and working collaboratively with someone else makes a powerful contribution to how a child's skills develop.

"Two Wrongs Can Make a Right"

One of the striking things about childhood is the amount of time children spend playing together, collaborating on games and sharing the task of solving problems. Even when neither one starts out with any particular expertise, pairs of children can be much more successful in solving a problem than a child working alone.[4] To some extent, this is undoubtedly because each child can make just that little contribution the partner would not have thought of otherwise. But we are beginning to identify a range of complex processes that help children to learn better from working collaboratively.

Two children collaborating on a problem may have different levels of understanding of the problem itself, or different background knowledge and assumptions. This can lead to a conflict of views, in which one child's perceptions and strategy directly challenge and stretch the other's. Willem Doise and his collaborators suggested that such conflicts should put powerful pressure on children to change their conceptions and develop new strategies.[5] Conflict of this kind between perspectives is just what Jean Piaget believed to be essential for real change in a child's skills.[6]

Collaborations between children with different approaches can certainly be productive. But it does not seem to be the *conflict* between views per se that is critical in determining whether a collaboration is productive or fruitless. Rather, it is the *form* of the interaction between the collaborators. "Two wrongs can make a right," the quotation that heads this section, comes from a study by Martin Glachan and Paul Light, who looked at how pairs of children collaborated with one another in solving problems.[7] Often, the two collaborators would each bring a different strategy to the problem, neither one necessarily the best. If they could find a way to share the decision-making as they addressed the problem, they could learn a new, more sophisticated strategy than either individual had devised to begin with. A pair working together in this way is more likely to discover a better strategy than either individual would working alone.

The way such collaborations work is this: The shared decisions are influenced by the two different strategies the children have brought to the task. The children jointly agree on moves that neither would have thought of on his or her own. This effectively disrupts both children's original strategies and, through processes similar to those discussed in Chapter 4, opens up the range of feedback available to them. New feedback brings the possibility of new discoveries and of movement toward a strategy more effectively focused on the problem in hand. In effect, the interaction between two wrong strategies can speed up the discovery of the right one.

Not all collaborations between children are so fruitful. Sometimes children with different strategies simply cannot find a way to share decisions. Perhaps their differing strategies are too much in conflict to allow any agreement over what to try, or perhaps the individual children cannot find a way to take account of each other's opinions. If there is no joint decision-making, the children do not gain much from working together. What typically happens is that one child dominates, leaving the other with nothing to do but watch passively. The dominant children in such partnerships are, in effect, problem-solving by themselves, and make (or don't make) exactly the same discoveries they would have made working alone.

Passive children in such lopsided partnerships, however, do sometimes gain: if the dominant partner has the better strategy, the passive spectator can sometimes learn from the experience. The key factor seems to be whether passive partners have a chance to work out conflicts between the understanding and expectations that come from their own strategy and the feedback that comes from the strategy the dominant partner is pursuing. Willem Doise has found that in problems like the Tower of Hanoi, in which problem-solving focuses on physical activity, the dominant partner can be so much in control of the action that the passive partner has no chance to understand what is going on, and so, no chance to learn from the experience.[8] But with other kinds of problems the dominant children may explain their strategy and thus give their partner a chance to understand the task and interpret the feedback from it. So long as the dominant child is using the better strategy, the passive partner can learn something useful.

Learning by Joining In

The Russian psychologist Lev Vygotsky proposed that the process of joining in some activity, particularly the experience of sharing problem-solving with a skilled partner, is one of the major ways through which children acquire their skills.[9] Vygotsky showed that the level of skill a child can produce is very much a matter of how much support the child has from the environment—especially from other people. For instance, a three-year-old may be quite successful in packing a suitcase for an overnight stay with a parent's help but quite unable to make an appropriate plan, or to complete the task effectively, by herself. The adult's help structures the task and guides the child, allowing her to do something that is beyond her individual capacity. Vygotsky argued that by stretching the child's efforts in this way, the adult allows the child both the opportunity and the means for developing new skills. As the child masters more, the adult can give less support until the child is able to manage the problem successfully on her own.

James Wertsch provides a good description of this process through an account of how a young child learns to solve jigsaw puzzles by sharing the activity with a parent.[10] At first, the child has no conception of what a jigsaw puzzle is, still less any idea of how to go about completing one. The parent explains the activity, suggesting that solving jigsaw puzzles is fun. The first few times they tackle a jigsaw together, almost all the activity comes from the parent: the adult works through the puzzle, spreading the pieces out, commenting on what needs doing, searching for the next piece, showing how it snaps into place—and encouraging the child to join in. At this stage, the child may do little more than perhaps snap in a few pieces in positions the parent has suggested. The way this sort of interaction develops is familiar to most parents and teachers: as the child's grasp of the puzzle improves, the adult's contribution gradually lessens, and the child takes on more and more of the problem-solving. The child begins to join in the search for the right pieces, while the parent offers suggestions or clues ("Do you think this could be the right piece?" or "How about if you try that piece up the other way?") in place of the more direct instructions given to the absolute beginner ("Try this piece . . . turn it up the other way"). For an older, more experienced child, the adult might do no more than offer general advice ("You could have another look at the picture on the box . . . why don't you leave that bit and come back to it when you've done the easy parts?" and so on).

What is going on here is that, initially, the parent is providing all the problem-solving skill the child lacks—from identifying the goal right through to shaping the details of the solution. The interaction between the child and the adult allows the child to join in and solve a problem way beyond his or her individual grasp. Because the adult is providing so much support, the child is free to learn a little here and a little there, without having to worry about the overall problem all at one time. By withdrawing support in stages when the child is ready to take over, the adult helps the child expand what he or she can do and stretch toward mastering the whole process of solving jigsaws.

Jerome Bruner and David Wood have given symbiotic interactions of this kind the evocative name "scaffolding."[11] Children learn many skills through such scaffolded support from an adult. But the child in Wertsch's example is not just learning about the specific skills of solving jigsaw puzzles; symbiotic relationships like this also teach children more general skills. Parents who interrupt their puzzle-solving to reflect on what to do next or to evaluate their progress are also teaching the child to plan and to monitor how successful their problem-solving has been so far. Children can learn such things as how to cope with persistent difficulties (give up? lay the pieces aside and come back to them later? carry on until it's fixed?) by cooperating with others in such situations.

Parents seem to be naturally disposed toward symbiotic, scaffolded interactions with their children. Stuart McNaughton and Jane Leyland,[12] for example, found that mothers helping their three-year-olds to solve jigsaw puzzles adapt the amount of support they provide to reflect the difficulty of the task or the skills of the child; they give more help when the task is harder or when a child struggles more with the problem. But even so, parents differ in how effectively they "scaffold" their child's problem-solving.[13]

Vygotsky's work suggests that scaffolded relationships are most effective when the parent provides enough support to stretch the child's problem-solving just the right amount: far enough to let the child achieve something new, which he or she could not have done alone, but not so far that the child cannot comprehend or learn from the experience.[14] Vygotsky called this optimal area the "zone of proximal development," in other words, the area of skill the child is ready to master next. Children learn most from experiences of shared problem-solving that take them beyond their existing skill and into this new area. It seems that some parents—and presumably some teachers too—are better than others at creating scaffolds that take an individual child into the zone where he or she will learn the most.

Success in building effective scaffolds for a child's emerging skills seems to be related to parents' tutoring style. Michael Pratt and his colleagues have found that the parents who provide the best scaffolds—and whose children learn the most as a consequence—are those who manage to combine sensitivity to the child's need for support and nurturance with a firm, demanding style of communicating and enforcing rules.[15]

Pratt's results fit very well with David Wood's study of mothers helping their four- to five-year-old children to build a pyramid (see Figure 24).[16] The task is quite difficult for children of this age: they must choose blocks of the right size and shape for each layer of the pyramid, put the blocks together in a particular order and orientation, and work through the layers in the right order. Few five-year-olds can manage this unaided. Wood identified five levels of support a parent might provide, increasing in the degree of directiveness and decreasing in the amount of responsibility left to the child as one goes down the list:

Level 1:   General verbal encouragement
Level 2:   Specific verbal instruction
Level 3:   Assists choice of material
Level 4:   Prepares material for assembly
Level 5:   Demonstrates an operation[17]

Children whose mothers simply demonstrated the problem-solving did not learn much from this task. Equally,

Figure 24

children whose mothers did not point or demonstrate, but relied on verbal instructions, did not learn much: they were not successful in solving the problem alone after the session with their mother. The mothers who taught their children the most were those who used both verbal instructions and demonstrations, and tailored the exact form of their help to the situation.[18] Such mothers might begin with a verbal suggestion but offer a demonstration if the child did not understand or could not follow it. In effect, they would respond to the child's difficulties by providing firmer direction and further demonstration. Once the child had grasped a point successfully, mothers with this successful tutoring style would let the child take the initiative. It is easy to see why this style is effective: it is very responsive to the child's immediate situation. By stepping in to help the child around difficulties, the mother circumvents anxiety and frustration, and by backing off when the child is more successful, she clears space for her child to explore and make discoveries.[19]

Barbara Rogoff has coined the name *guided participation* for successful scaffolding interactions like those identified by Wood and Pratt. She defines guided participation as a collaborative process in which adult and child share problem-solving, the adult explaining and supporting the child's efforts, but both the adult and child involved in the process of making decisions.[20] It is quite clear from Rogoff's research that these last two elements are critical if the child is to be able to learn from the interaction. Interacting with another child who happens to be expert in the task does not teach the child as much as interacting with an adult. Take, for example, the task of planning a route to various stores on a map (see Figure 25). Rogoff tested what nine-year-old children would learn if they tackled this task with a peer who had previously been trained to complete the task expertly, or

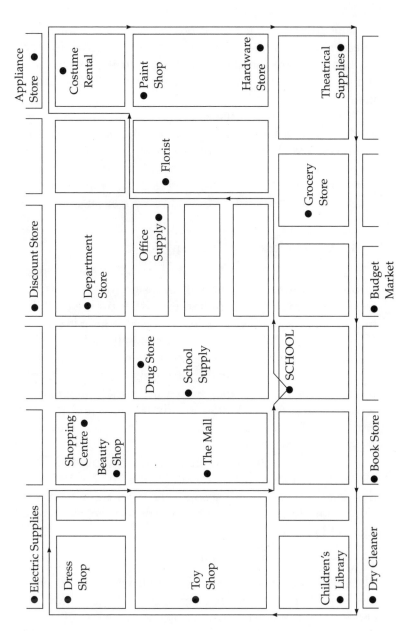

Figure 25

with an adult partner.[21] Children learned more from their interaction with the adult. The expert child does not explain or share the decision-making to the extent that the adult does. Simply demonstrating a skilled solution is not the best way to teach.

Of course, it is not just young children who learn by joining in with a more experienced problem-solver. Apprentices, whether in a trade, a science, or a sport, learn a great deal from working in collaboration with an expert and through the same processes: sharing decision-making and gradually taking on more responsibility.

Tasks and Contexts in Teaching Skills

It is much easier to teach children to solve some kinds of problems than it is others. It is easier, for example, to teach them to handle familiar, everyday problems than to deal with the kinds of problems they encounter in school work. Virtually all normal ten-year-olds have learned to navigate their way around their own community, though many may have problems interpreting maps in a geography lesson. Or a child who can work out what is wrong with a roller skate—and fix it—may find it very hard to understand the same principles when they are taught in a physics lesson.

Why are some things easier to teach than others? Two factors seem to have a crucial effect: first, the kind of skill that is to be taught; and second, the extent to which the skill is taught in the context of purposes and meanings the child can understand.

The Kind of Skill to Be Taught

The easiest problem-solving skills to teach are the everyday skills the child needs over and over again: how to choose what to wear, how to use a particular piece of equipment, how to fix a snack, and so on. With recurring problems like this, we can teach the child quite specific, concrete skills: rules for matching clothes to events, for example, or precise recipes for baking cookies or for operating a microwave oven. The child can develop a body of experience with a given problem and then can draw on this and on analogy, rather than on more abstract or analytical skills, in facing new versions of the problem. Concrete problem-solving skills are much the easiest to teach and to learn.

The hardest kind of skills to teach are those in which the child must learn to apply an abstract principle or to analyze a situation and construct a strategy from scratch. Many of the things we want children to learn in school are of this kind: the child must learn the abstract *principle* of writing a poem, not a specific procedure for writing any one particular poem. Or the child might have to learn to apply general principles in designing an experiment in physics. In teaching this kind of skill, showing the child concrete examples of what to do is not enough. Children do learn to abstract principles from concrete examples for themselves, as Jerome Bruner and Helen Kenney's study (described in Chapter 2) shows.[22] But learning an abstract principle from concrete examples is hard, and it takes time. Helping a child to do this is a more subtle and complex process than teaching a concrete skill.

Purposes and Meanings

It is easier to teach children in contexts where they understand and share the goals that motivate problem-solving than in contexts where the goal seems meaningless or incomprehensible.[23] Meaningful purposes motivate children. They provide a structure for the use of skills that is simply not present when the child cannot understand the reason for the activity. The same is just as true for adults. Imagine yourself on a beach. Someone asks you to help dig out a large bank of soil from the cliff and insists that it must be done with bare hands, not shovels. Your response is likely to be very much affected by the reason you are given for doing it: that is, you are more likely to work hard, to follow instructions carefully, and to figure out better ways of approaching the problem if you are told that a child is buried under the bank than if the task is proposed as a game with no real purpose.

The commitment children show to solving problems whose purpose they understand is an important factor in their success. Whether they are working toward a goal they have set for themselves or on a chore with an obviously desirable target (like changing a plug to make the TV work), seeing the point of achieving the goal motivates them not only to persist but to pay attention to the details of the problem, both key factors in learning.

Problems with a real purpose offer further advantages. The reason for tackling a problem also plays an important role in structuring the process of solving it. For example, if a child helps in fixing the lock to the front door of the house, the importance of the activity is apparent. At the same time, the purpose defines the character of the solution: the problem is not fixed until the lock will hold the door shut. Solutions that would restore the lock's appearance, such as gluing the broken pieces together, can be easily identified as wrong. The glue is too weak to hold. Solutions that produce a strange-looking lock, like improvised levers made by bending the remains of the original ones, are right if they do the job. If the child were mending an old lock for no particular reason, there would be no basis for choosing between a cosmetic fix and an ugly but functional one.

We are only just beginning to explore the ways in

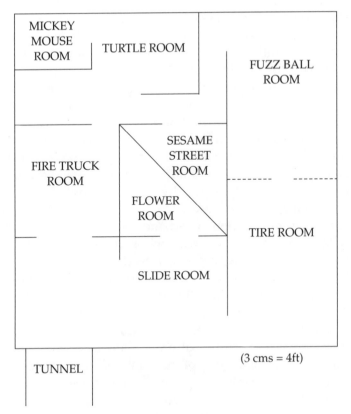

MICKEY MOUSE ROOM

TURTLE ROOM

FUZZ BALL ROOM

FIRE TRUCK ROOM

SESAME STREET ROOM

FLOWER ROOM

TIRE ROOM

SLIDE ROOM

TUNNEL

(3 cms = 4ft)

Figure 26

which purposes structure goals in children's problem-solving. But some studies have already produced striking illustrations. Mary Gauvain and Barbara Rogoff asked children of six to nine years old to play in a specially built "funhouse," in which there were a number of rooms, each decorated in a different and distinctive way (see Figure 26).[24] Some of the rooms (for example, the flower room) were "dead ends": you had to go back out the same way you came in. Other rooms (for example, the slide room) were "passageways" leading from one area to another. Half of the children were asked to explore the funhouse until they had a good understanding of the best path for making their way through it without getting stuck anywhere. The other half were asked to explore until they had a good grasp of the overall layout. After playing in the funhouse, each child was asked questions to establish how well he or she could recall the route between two points and the overall layout of the space. Both groups of children remembered the routes through the funhouse equally accurately, but those who had been specifically asked to explore the layout remembered far more about dead-end rooms and about the relative position of rooms, such as the "Sesame Street" room and the flower room. In effect, the *purpose* motivating the child's exploration affected the information the child gathered, and how that information was structured and could later be used.

Evidence of how purposes structure our problem-solving comes from studies of other skills too. There is the salutary story of a study of the ability of Kpelle tribesmen to sort objects into categories.[25] The tribesmen sorted things into functional categories (putting a hoe with a potato) rather than making the more taxonomic categories researchers expected mature adults to make (putting the hoe with other tools and the potato with other foods). The tribesmen justified their actions by saying these were the sortings a wise man would make. When the experimenter asked them what sorting a fool would make, they produced the taxonomic categories the experimenter had expected in the first place! The reason for making the classification determined the way the Kpelle solved the problem. This same phenomenon has also been described in many other situations:[26] for both adults and children all over the world, everyday classifications are functional rather than taxonomic or logical. When we organize a closet shelf, a dresser drawer, or even a kitchen cupboard, we put things where they will be most useful, making groupings that are practical rather than consistent. Only classifications made for the sake of making classifications are exhaustive, complete, or logical. Because it defines the goal, the purpose behind a problem can serve as the linchpin around which problem-solving skills are organized.

The purpose of a task also plays a fundamental role in bringing skills to bear in another way. Often, in solving a problem, we are not aware of the possible skills we might use. Rather, the appropriate skill comes to mind as we recognize what the goal is: it is stored in the context of that purpose and associated with solving problems of that type. When problem-solving is detached from familiar or comprehensible purposes, the very processes by which children retrieve skills from memory is disrupted.

Some researchers, such as Margaret Donaldson,[27] believe that there is little difference between young children and adults in their ability to learn to bring problem-solving skills to bear in situations where there is a clear and comprehensible purpose to the task. Where children have difficulty is in those situations where skills have to be exercised for their own sake—called forth from memory without any of the usual cues and prompts. How does the child develop the ability to decontextualize skills in this way, to detach them from their original purposes and use them as ends in themselves? Formal schooling is the key factor in this process.[28] Schools ask children to solve a great many problems, from learning to multiply large numbers to memorizing vast bodies of facts or translating from one language to another. No one explains why these skills are useful or what the point of learning them might be. Children themselves often complain about this ("What's the point of learning Latin? The Romans are all dead"; "I don't need to learn all this math stuff, I've got a calculator"—two protests recently heard in my house). Children quickly pick up on the fact that such complaints are considered irrelevant: what matters in school is learning to produce skills on demand in order to pass tests that show how well one can do it. In effect, what schooling gives the child is repeated practice in using skills outside any functional context.

Confidence and Control

There is something very special about learning to solve a problem in a social context. A toddler helping a parent to mend a broken lock is likely to feel a strong pride in the achievement and a sense of belonging, of having contributed to an activity that really matters to the parent. Success in solving problems—and other people's belief in our success—makes us feel competent and confident at any age. Children especially need that kind of confidence if they are to become good problem-solvers.

A study by Robert Hartley shows just how much impact confidence—or the lack of it—can have on children's problem-solving.[29] He looked at how a group of disadvantaged children normally solved problems: they were impulsive, they did not plan things effectively or monitor how well things were going, and they did not go back and correct their mistakes. Hartley asked these children to solve the same kind of problems again, but this time, they were to pretend to be the brightest child in the class and do things the way that child would. The children instantly became less impulsive, more planful, and began to notice and correct their mistakes. And they were far more successful in solving the problems!

Hartley discussed the test with the children afterwards.

One child's interview illustrates how his low opinion of himself undermined his usual problem-solving:

Adult: Do you usually do better than the person you acted like or worse?

Child: Worse.

Adult: Why?

Child: Because I'm Paul Hanworth.

This child clearly had skills he did not normally use because he did not think of himself as good at solving that type of problem. He had concluded that he was not as able as his peers, and that social information was holding him back.

Other studies underline the impact of children's experience of failure on their subsequent success in solving problems. The effect can be very powerful. If we give a group of twelve-year-olds anagrams to solve—half of the children quite easy anagrams and the other half impossible ones—we will find that there is a marked difference between the two groups in their later success in solving a fairly easy anagram like "hirac." The children who had successfully solved a number of anagrams earlier will be much more successful than those who experienced a depressing failure. This phenomenon is called "learned helplessness."[30] Some researchers have found that even relatively short episodes of being unsuccessful in one particular task can measurably lower a child's school achievement in other types of task for a while.

Studies like these suggest that children's problem-solving could be improved if parents and other adults could help them be more confident about their own abilities. But this is easier said than done.[31] It is very difficult to convince children that they are better at some skill than they actually are. Children are sharply aware of their own ranking in the classroom or among their siblings. They know who comes top in tests in each subject and who gets a parent's praise for solving problems at home. This sort of awareness is almost impossible to suppress, even in progressive schools, which put a lot of effort into playing down any sort of competition between children. An adult who tries to persuade children who rank very low in their science class that they are competent at science runs the risk of being patronizing and is unlikely to convince. The best one could hope for is to help the child not to feel bad about coming in last. This almost certainly brings many benefits, but it is not very likely to lead a child to get much better at solving problems in science classes.

Schools and parents have often tried to get around this problem by doing things to raise the child's morale and self-esteem in general. Many teachers, for example, believe that experiencing some success in sports can build an overall confidence that will spill over and help the child to tackle problems in other areas. But this does not work very well. Children base their confidence about their skills on their experiences with those skills, so confidence is tied quite closely to particular types of problem-solving.[32] A boy may know that he is good at spelling and at sports, but at the same time be worried about his poor skills in science or math. There is little reason why children should reevaluate their prowess in science just because they have become more confident in their athletic abilities.

Children pick up messages about their competence all the time, not just in school. Children whose offers to help at home are impatiently brushed aside learn that their help is not valued, that other people do not expect them to make a useful contribution or to be able to manage the task. They conclude that they are not competent. The proud three-year-old who has been invited to help—even if only by holding the tools or putting a finger just so when asked—gets a very different message. The way we decide whether to let a child help with or tackle a particular problem can play an important part in determining whether that child grows into a confident individual who expects to manage, to be able to solve problems, or one who is too anxiously insecure or too sure of failure even to try.

The powerful impact that confidence, or the lack of it, can have on a child's problem-solving and the difficulty of improving a child's self-confidence in helpful ways pose a problem for teacher and parent. Perhaps the best we can do here is to bias our reactions in the direction of providing the most positive feedback possible—praising what can be praised and offering criticism only constructively, and lightly. Studies of the relationship between different styles of parenting certainly support this approach: children who are highly successful problem-solvers tend to have parents who praise more and criticize less.[33]

Growing at Their Own Pace?

Just how much do social processes determine children's progress toward expert problem-solving? Are there constraints on what a child can learn from other people at any given point?

Of course, it is painfully obvious that there are indeed limits on what children of different ages can be taught. We can teach eight-year-olds to use a cross-product rule for balance scale tasks not normally mastered until the age of seventeen, but we would be lucky indeed to teach them fourth order differential equations. We can teach a three-year-old the letters of the alphabet, but usually not the rules of chess. We can teach an eighteen-month-old to roll out cookie dough and cut out shapes, but not to prepare a complex casserole or cross a road in safety, and so on.

Building on What You Know

Where do these limits on what a child can be taught come from? In part, they reflect what the child already knows. Almost every piece of knowledge or skill that we have presupposes, and rests on, some other piece of knowledge or skill: You cannot begin to understand algebra if you do not know that letters of the alphabet can represent unknown numerical quantities. You cannot learn to tap dance if you have not yet mastered walking. At some level, we have known this for a long time. Many researchers, from learning theorists to Jean Piaget, whose approach is very different, to more recent thinkers in the field, have all emphasized that children cannot be expected to learn something unless they already have the appropriate background knowledge and skills.[34]

This point is so obvious that no teacher or parent is likely to disagree—in principle. But in practice, trouble can arise because adults are not always good at identifying what an individual child already knows, or articulating what he or she needs to know, to master some new skill. We forget that a concept (such as "alive") may mean one thing to a three-year-old and something quite different to a thirteen-year-old; or that a five-year-old and an eight-year-old may attend to quite different aspects of a task (as in the balance scale task) even though they may use the same strategy in solving it. We set out with the best of intentions, but few parents or teachers can honestly say that they have never left a child more confused than he or she was before being "helped." Too often we forget that, while such failures may leave the adult frustrated (or even irritated), they often leave the child anxious and upset. Responsibility for the failure ought to lie with the adult, but it is too often felt only by the child.

Determining what an individual child already understands in some problem-solving situation can be difficult. Children are often too confused to be able to say exactly what they need to have explained again or too shy to say they have not understood. For a parent or a teacher, there is little to go on but commonsense expectations, and we can easily get it wrong. What would we need to teach children to enable them to solve the problem of constructing a self-assembly bookcase on the basis of the manufacturer's instructions? All the elements of the problem (the various parts of the bookcase and the required hardware) are given, and the instructions ostensively provide a complete plan of the work. One manufacturer in England actually boasts that all its products can be assembled by a child of twelve, yet many grown people are perplexed, frustrated, and sometimes defeated by such tasks. Why? In cases like these, the instructions often presuppose skills and experience so obvious to those who write them that they see no need to explain, but which the rest of us do not possess. Parents—and teachers—can sometimes underestimate the complexity of what a child will need to learn to master each new step in problem-solving, and produce confusion and misunderstanding as a consequence.

In fact, we are only just beginning to realize exactly how much background information is involved in any problem-solving skill. So much of what a human being knows is tacit, implicit in other things, or taken for granted—and thus effectively invisible. Only when we try to program a computer to simulate human problem-solving—to learn a new concept or use a particular strategy—do we confront in detail the full extent and complexity of the knowledge required for these things.

Opportunities to Learn

What children already know and what is demanded for the next step are not the only constraints on the speed at which they learn to solve various kinds of problems. Opportunities for learning also have a major effect: how can you master chess if you have never seen the game, or solve the problem of mending a broken alarm clock unless you try?

To some extent, the physical environment constrains children's opportunities for tackling particular kinds of problems. All children interact with, and so have the opportunity to learn about, such fundamental phenomena as gravity. But different environments mean that individual children will inevitably have different opportunities to observe and participate in problem-solving of any given type. For example, children living in houses with large yards and gardens can try their hand at solving the problems involved in building a shelter or a fort, like the two boys in Chapter 1. Those living in apartments, however, will have fewer opportunities for games of this type, and thus, fewer opportunities to learn how to tackle the problems that arise.

But as researchers such as Barbara Rogoff, Mary Gauvain, and Shari Ellis have pointed out, children's opportunities to address different kinds of problems are controlled primarily by adults—by their parents and their teachers.[35] We shape the lives of children and students by controlling their experience in order to avoid problems we believe too difficult for them, and steering them toward the activities we think appropriate for their age and abilities.

Of course, controlling children's exposure to different kinds of problems in this way is to some extent a natural part of the scaffolding process we saw earlier. But Rogoff and her colleagues point out that the choices we make about what activities our children encounter are not wholly driven by the child's own needs and abilities:[36] the adults in one culture may have quite different expectations than those in another about what is appropriate for a child of a given age, and they will provide their children with quite different opportunities for mastering problem-solving as a consequence. In Europe and North America, for example, girls of ten or eleven years old are still children and do not marry. The idea that they might cope with the problems of housekeeping or motherhood would seem absurd to their parents. But in other cultures, girls of this age do marry, and are expected to deal with the problems of domestic life. An eight-year-old Nigerian boy might be dispatched with the family's herd of cattle or goats and be expected to deal with the problems of finding water and grazing, or fending off predators. His contemporaries in Britain or the United States are scarcely trusted to wash the dishes, let alone take sole responsibility for the family's main asset, although 150 years ago these children might have worked down a coal mine or in a factory. Rogoff has identified cultural differences in what we expect of children right through from infancy to adulthood.[37] In Western societies, most babies are weaned from the breast by six months—which to most African mothers would seem a brutally young age to force a child to cope with this loss. Around the world, the average age for weaning is two-and-a-half. In most cultures, puberty is the beginning of adult life, with all its responsibilities and rights. In Western cultures, adolescents are still treated as children. Yet despite the differences between cultures, children live up to the expectations of the society around them, more or less. Indian and African children behave as their societies expect them to, as do French and American children.

Rogoff's studies of how adult control over children's opportunities to explore different kinds of problems determines the pattern and pace of their development are fascinating. To the extent that such processes operate, the factors that determine the development of problem-solving skill are as much social as cognitive.

6 / Conclusions

Chapter 1 posed several questions about the origins of the child's growing expertise in solving problems. Does it come from basic changes in mental skills, in the very ability to reason, as the child grows older? If so, exactly how do these skills change? Or is the growth of problem-solving more a matter of practice, of learning to apply skills successfully in new contexts? Just what do children do when they try to solve problems and how do they get better at it? As we have seen, the answers to these questions are complex. The research reviewed in this book shows how our understanding of the issues has evolved over the past twenty years—and is still evolving.

The Nature of the Child's Developing Skills

Jean Piaget suggested that logical structures were the essential base on which problem-solving depends.[1] For Piaget, the child's growing mastery of problem-solving reflected an increasing sophistication in logical skill, which develops through regular stages. At any one stage, the child's reasoning is characterized by a particular kind of logic, and has the same quality, more or less, across different kinds of task. But this view has been severely challenged by other lines of research. First, as we saw in Chapter 2, even adult reasoning does not draw on logical skill to anything like the extent Piaget assumed. If adults do not rely on logic to solve problems, how can we interpret children's progress toward adult reasoning as a matter of increasing logical skill? Second, children's skills vary from one situation to another much more than one would expect if these skills depended on abstract, general processes such as logic.

The discovery of variation in skill from one context to another has radically changed our understanding of what is involved in problem-solving. Instead of being driven by abstract skills like logic, problem-solving draws deeply on knowledge of the particular concrete detail of the task in hand. What you know about a task determines how you plan to tackle the problem, what strategies you consider, and how you interpret feedback, as we saw in Chapter 3. Increased understanding makes new kinds of mental tools, such as principled inferences, available to the child. The theories and expectations children build up about a given type of problem determine what analogies they can draw, and so, what skills they can recognize as relevant or can bring to bear.

Expertise in problem-solving grows out of the child's expanding knowledge and experience of particular types of problems. Because skill is so tightly tied to knowledge of a particular task or domain, problem-solving expertise can develop at different paces in different contexts. This is why a child—or an adult—can be a skilled problem-solver in one context but a complete novice in another. The child starts out as a novice in all types of problem-solving and gradually develops expertise through the experience.

From this new perspective, many of the things that once seemed so puzzling about children's problem-solving now start to make sense. For example, in some situations, even very young children can surprise us with their skill as problem-solvers. In other situations, much older children surprise us with their failures. But our surprise comes only from our false assumption that problem-solving skill ought to be consistent across different tasks or across different versions of the same task. Once we abandon that assumption, we are free to look more closely at the situations in which younger and older children succeed or fail, and to discover that the patterns of variation we see in children's success and failure are not really surprising at all.

Very young infants are far more capable than we have supposed. They are born with the tools and interests they need to interact with others and learn from and about the world. So it should not surprise us if an infant's problem-solving in areas such as interpreting facial expressions, where the child is likely to have an innate predisposition to build on, is quite sophisticated. Success in this domain need have no implications for the infant's problem-solving in areas that are of less instinctive interest or relevance.

Similarly, it is not surprising that the six-year-old seems so adept a problem-solver in some areas of everyday life, but is unsophisticated in most experimental tests of problem-solving, in schoolwork, and the like. Such a child may be an expert, as it were, in relation to some familiar kinds of problem, but a novice with respect to others. Since problem-solving success depends on rich representations of the problem and on possible solutions associated with expert knowledge, we should not expect children to be consistent in solving problems across all areas.

A striking aspect of the differences between younger and older problem-solvers is that the older ones are often quicker to learn in some new context, or quicker to work out how to solve a problem for themselves. This is not always true, of course, as most adults who lived through the craze of Rubik's cube or who are currently struggling with their children's Nintendo computer games will know. And sometimes there is a child prodigy who masters complex problems better than most adults could: Mozart, for example, producing brilliant performances at the age of five. These instances of reversed age effect might well reflect the fact that prodigies, and games buffs, will attend to their chosen area for many hours, days, weeks, and even months. Few adults have either the opportunity or the inclination to put in so much time or effort.

Generally, that older individuals learn and solve problems more quickly should not surprise us if we reflect on the fact that the older individual is more likely to have richer knowledge than the young child, and not just in one area but in many. Knowledge is cumulative, not simply in the sense that one step in understanding a particular problem depends on another, but also in the sense that richer knowledge in one area allows an individual to see more connections between different areas. As we noted in relation to the child's ability to use analogies, the more knowledge an individual has, the more analogies he or she will be able to draw—and to use—in solving problems or in organizing and learning new material. Rich knowledge across many areas broadens the range of analogies that can be considered in addressing a new problem and thus increases the chances of finding a helpful way to represent what needs to be done. The increasing ability to transfer skills from situation to situation is a powerful thing indeed: the more analogies you can recognize, the more likely it is that you can behave planfully, even in unfamiliar situations.

Some theorists, such as Jerry Fodor and Howard Gardner, have suggested that the fact that problem-solving skill is so tied to domain-specific knowledge reflects the underlying structure of intelligence.[2] They suggest that human intelligence is divided up into many different compartments or "modules" in one way or another. Gardner, for example, suggests that children have one type of intelligence for mathematical problems, a second for musical problems, a third for linguistic reasoning, and so on. These various "intelligences" are different in kind from one another, and develop and operate quite separately and independently, each drawing on its own special kind of process.

Ideas like Gardner's are intriguing but controversial. There are, for example, some kinds of process that seem to operate across all sorts of different domains. I described some of these in Chapter 4. The processes by which a child chooses a strategy in tackling a new problem, adjusts that strategy in the light of feedback, or discovers new strategies seem to be fundamentally the same in many different domains. Other theorists have criticized Fodor and Gardner, arguing that processes like these could not operate so generally if intelligence were really compartmentalized into separate modules for each type of skill.[3]

An alternative interpretation of the relationship between domain-specific knowledge and general processes can be simply represented through the metaphor of a food processor. There may be a single set of machinery for planning problem-solving, selecting strategies, devising new ones, and so on (the food processor), through which many different kinds of specific knowledge (the foodstuffs) are processed. The food processor needs foodstuffs to operate. But just how it operates and what it produces depend on what is put into it. A mixture of flour and fat has its own distinctive character and blends together at its own distinctive pace, and it comes out looking and tasting quite different from a mixture of bananas and milk, say, although both have gone through the same process. What you put into the machine determines how the machine operates and what comes out; the machine itself stays the same.

Malleable Skills

Piaget believed that there was little scope for improving the young child's problem-solving.[4] Real change in a child's skills depended on the construction of new logical structures in the child's mind, and adults—and the social world as a whole—could have only a limited role in this process. Logical understanding had to be built by processes internal to the child. Each individual child had to do this at his or her own pace and could not be hurried along.

The research I have described in this book suggests a very different picture. Change and growth in problem-solving skill reflect increasing information and experience. Given the right opportunities and experiences, quite striking changes can occur in a relatively short time. Far from being helpless to influence development, social interactions play a critical role in the child's progress: skills are transmitted through social interactions, particularly through sharing the process of problem-solving with a more skilled adult; and the social world structures and controls the child's access to opportunities to gain new expertise.

Just how malleable are the child's skills? Could every child be as expert at a given type of problem-solving as the best if he or she had the right opportunities and experiences? We don't yet know. The question is closely related to the problem of why there are such clear individual differences between one child and another, both in their skill as problem-solvers and in their attitudes to tackling problems. Why is it that Lesley is so very much more successful than her brother in almost every area of problem-solving? Why is she faster to make new discoveries or to adopt a new strategy? Why does she seek out opportunities to tackle fresh problems, while her brother avoids them at all costs? The research we have looked at here offers some clues: Lesley may be quicker to recognize that a strategy is associated with success, in the way Siegler described,[5] and so may be able to learn faster, from less experience, than her brother can. Or she may happen to have been luckier and selected strategies that were more fruitful in yielding new discoveries than her brother did, and so have been more successful and gained more confidence. Perhaps she had better experiences of sharing problem-solving with her parents or more opportunities to do so than her brother.

As yet, no one has fully worked through the question of the origins of individual differences in problem-solving. Can we fully explain such effects in terms of the factors we have already identified in exploring the development of problem-solving skills, or are there other, perhaps more genetically fixed factors involved as well?

New Directions

Recent research has explained a great deal about the fascinating and varied phenomena of children's problem-solving. It has made sense of many issues that seemed separate and disjointed before and given us new ways of interpreting what we see in our everyday interactions with children.

Of course, there are many interesting questions to which we still have no answer, such as how general skills and specific knowledge fit together and where individual differences in skill come from. But that is the nature of research: there will always be another question to answer, and each new discovery opens up new questions.

For me, the biggest mystery of all is still the question I posed at the beginning: why is problem-solving sometimes such fun? That is, why do human beings go looking for problems to solve instead of just doing the things we can already do? What function does problem-solving serve to make it so attractive and to justify its fundamental role in childhood activities? In a real sense, problem-solving is at the heart of what we mean by intelligence. The ability to identify a goal, work out how to achieve it, and carry out that plan is the essence of every intelligent activity. But the core of problem-solving is also that it produces change: in the child's understanding of the task, in the strategy the child uses to deal with it, and so on. Could it be that the processes of solving problems are so fundamental because they provide the very machinery and motor producing cognitive development itself?

This last issue is the next major question in understanding problem-solving. Some theorists have argued that problem-solving processes are powerful and pervasive enough to produce all the conceptual growth and change we see through childhood. Others, most notably Piaget, have argued that this is not so, and that there must be other, endogenous processes more specifically focused on yielding developmental change. Is this controversy just a matter of definition? The answer will depend on what we choose to include in the category "problem-solving processes." But the real challenge is an empirical one: can we fully explain all the changes in children's skills and understanding through processes like those I have described? Answering this question sets the agenda for the next step forward in understanding cognitive development.

Notes

1 / WHY CHILDREN'S PROBLEM-SOLVING IS INTERESTING

1. J. Piaget, *Genetic Epistemology* (New York: Columbia University Press, 1968).
2. L. Vygotsky, *Thought and Language* (Cambridge, Mass.: MIT Press, 1962).

2 / A HISTORICAL PERSPECTIVE ON CHILDREN'S PROBLEM-SOLVING

1. J. Bruner, *Beyond the Information Given* (London: Allen and Unwin, 1974).
2. J. Piaget, *Genetic Epistemology* (New York: Columbia University Press, 1968).
3. M. Donaldson, *Children's Minds* (Glasgow: Collins/Fontana, 1978).
4. Ibid.
5. R. Gelman, "Cognitive Development," *Annual Review of Psychology* 29 (1980): 297–332.
6. Donaldson, *Children's Minds*.
7. J. St. B. Evans, J. L. Barstow, and P. Pollard, "On the Conflict between Logic and Belief in Syllogistic Reasoning," *Memory and Cognition* 11 (1983): 295–306.
8. G. Potts, "Storing and Retrieving Information about Or-

dered Relationships," *Journal of Experimental Psychology* 103 (1974): 431–439.

9. P. Wason and P. Johnson-Laird, *Psychology of Reasoning: Structure and Content* (London: Batsford, 1972).

10. P. Cheng and K. Holyoak, "Pragmatic Reasoning Schemas," *Cognitive Psychology* 17 (1985): 391–416.

11. P. Johnson-Laird, *Mental Models* (Cambridge, Mass.: Harvard University Press, 1983).

12. P. Johnson-Laird, J. Oakhill, and D. Bull, "Children's Syllogistic Reasoning," *Quarterly Journal of Experimental Psychology* 38A (1986): 35–58.

13. J. Bruner and H. Kenney, "Representation and Mathematical Learning," *Monograph of the Society for Research in Child Development* 30(1) (1965): 50–59.

14. Donaldson, *Children's Minds.*

15. A. Luria, *The Social History of Cognition* (Cambridge, Mass.: Harvard University Press, 1977); M. Cole and S. Scribner, *Culture and Thought: A Psychological Introduction* (New York: Wiley, 1974).

16. J. Hawkins, R. Pea, J. Glick, and S. Scribner, "'Merds That Laugh Don't Like Mushrooms': Evidence for Deductive Reasoning by Preschoolers," *Developmental Psychology* 20 (1984): 595–606.

3 / CONCEPTUAL TOOLS FOR SOLVING PROBLEMS

1. J. Piaget, *Genetic Epistemology* (New York: Columbia University Press, 1968); J. Locke, *An Essay Concerning Human Understanding*, ed. P. H. Nidditch (Oxford: Clarendon Press, 1975); originally published in 1690.

2. K. Wynn, "Children's Understanding of Counting," *Cognition* 36 (1990): 155–193.

3. R. M. Golinkoff, C. G. Harding, V. Carlson-Luden, and M. Sexton, "The Infant's Perception of Causal Events: The Distinction between Animate and Inanimate Objects," in *Advances in Infancy Research,* vol. 3, ed. L. Lipsett and C. K. Rovee-Collier (Norwood, N.J.: Ablex, 1984).

4. J. Mehler, G. Lambertz, P. Jisczyk, and C. Arniel-Tison, "Discrimination de la Longue Materielle par le Nouveau né,"

Comptes Rends Academie des Sciences 303, 3d ser. (1986): 637–640.

5. P. Kellman and E. Spelke, "Perception of Partly Occluded Objects in Infancy," *Cognitive Psychology* 15 (1983): 483–524.
6. D. Kahneman, P. Slovic, and A. Tversky, eds., *Judgment under Uncertainty: Heuristics and Biases* (Cambridge: Cambridge University Press, 1982).
7. Ibid.
8. E. Rosch, "Principles of Categorization," in *Cognition and Categorization,* ed. E. Rosch and B. Lloyd (Hillsdale, N.J.: Erlbaum, 1978).
9. Kahneman, Slovic, and Tversky, *Judgment under Uncertainty.*
10. L. Ross, "The 'Intuitive Scientist' Formulation and Its Developmental Implications," in *Social Cognitive Development: Frontiers and Possible Futures,* ed. J. H. Flavell and L. Ross (Cambridge: Cambridge University Press, 1981).
11. Piaget, *Genetic Epistemology.*
12. R. Siegler, "Three Aspects of Cognitive Development," *Cognitive Psychology* 8 (1976): 481–520.
13. Ibid.
14. S. Carey, *Conceptual Change in Childhood* (Cambridge, Mass., and London: MIT Press, 1985).
15. Ibid.
16. Ibid.
17. S. Gelman and E. Markman, "Categories and Induction in Young Children," *Cognition* 23 (1986): 183–209; S. Gelman and E. Markman, "Young Children's Inductions from Natural Kinds: The Role of Categories and Appearances," *Child Development* 58 (1987): 1532–1541.
18. L. Smith, "In Defence of Perceptual Similarity" (paper presented at the Biennial Meeting of the Society for Research in Child Development, Kansas City, 1989).
19. M. Chi, P. J. Feltovich, and R. Glaser, "Categorization and Representation of Physics Problems by Experts and Novices," *Cognitive Science* 5 (1981): 121–152.
20. J. H. Flavell and H. M. Wellman, "Metamemory," in *Perspectives on the Development of Memory and Cognition,* ed. R. V. Kail, Jr., and J. W. Hagen (Hillsdale, N.J.: Erlbaum, 1977).

21. B. Inhelder and J. Piaget, *The Growth of Logical Thinking from Childhood to Adolescence* (New York: Basic Books, 1958).
22. U. Goswami and A. Brown, "Melting Chocolate and Melting Snowmen: Analogical Reasoning and Causal Relations," *Cognition* 35 (1989): 69–95.
23. P. Willatts, "Development of Problem-Solving in Infancy," in *Infant Development,* ed. A. Slater and J. Bremner (London: Erlbaum, 1989).
24. W. Fabricius, "The Development of Forward Search in Preschoolers," *Child Development* 59 (1988): 1473–1488.
25. Willatts, "Development of Problem-Solving in Infancy."
26. D. Klahr and M. Robinson, "Formal Assessment of Problem-Solving and Planning Processes in Preschool Children," *Cognitive Psychology* 13 (1981): 113–148.
27. R. Case, "Intellectual Development from Birth to Adulthood: A Neo-Piagetian Interpretation", in *Children's Thinking: What Develops?* ed. R. Siegler (Hillsdale, N.J.: Erlbaum, 1978).
28. Ibid.
29. A. Brown and J. DeLoache, "Skills, Plans and Self-regulation," in *Children's Thinking: What Develops?* ed. Siegler.
30. A. Karmiloff-Smith, *Beyond Modularity: A Developmental Perspective on Cognitive Science* (Cambridge, Mass.: Bradford Books, MIT Press, 1992).
31. Ibid.
32. Ibid.
33. A. D. De Groot, *Thought and Choice in Chess* (The Hague: Mouton, 1965).
34. M. Chi, "Knowledge Structures and Memory Development," in *Children's Thinking: What Develops?* ed. Siegler.

4 / WORKING THROUGH A PROBLEM AND DISCOVERING NEW STRATEGIES

1. R. Siegler and E. Jenkins, *How Children Discover New Strategies* (Hillsdale, N.J.: Erlbaum, 1989); R. Siegler, "How Domain-General and Domain-Specific Knowledge Interact

to Produce Strategy Choices," *Merrill-Palmer Quarterly* 35 (1989): 1–26.

2. Siegler and Jenkins, *How Children Discover New Strategies.*

3. Ibid.

4. Ibid.

5. D. Klahr, "Transition Processes in Quantitative Development," in *Mechanisms of Cognitive Development*, ed. R. Sternberg (New York: Freeman, 1984); D. Klahr, "A Production System for Counting, Subitising and Adding," in *Visual Processing*, ed. W. Chase (New York: Academic Press, 1973).

6. A. Karmiloff-Smith, *Beyond Modularity: A Developmental Perspective on Cognitive Science* (Cambridge, Mass.: Bradford Books, MIT Press, 1992).

7. Ibid.

8. Siegler and Jenkins, *How Children Discover New Strategies.*

9. S. Thornton and H. Whitney, "Knowledge-Driven Change in Children's Problem-Solving," *Proceedings of the Sixth European Conference on Developmental Psychology*, Bonn, 1994; R. Wales and S. Thornton, "Psychological Issues in Modelling Creativity," in *Artificial Intelligence and Creativity*, ed. T. Dartnall (Dordrecht, The Netherlands: Kluwer, 1994).

10. E. Rosch, C. Mervis, W. Gray, D. Johnson, and P. Boyes-Bream, "Basic Objects in Natural Categories," *Cognitive Psychology* 8 (1976): 382–439.

5 / THE SOCIAL CONTEXT OF CHILDREN'S
PROBLEM-SOLVING

1. P. Light and A. Perret-Clermont, "Social Context Effects in Learning and Testing," in *Cognition and Social Worlds*, ed. A. Gellatly, D. Rogers, and J. Sloboda (Oxford: Clarendon Press, 1989).

2. Ibid.

3. Ibid.

4. W. Doise and G. Mugny, *The Social Development of the Intellect* (Oxford: Pergamon Press, 1984).

5. Ibid.; W. Doise and C. Hanselmann, "Conflict and Social

Marking in the Acquisition of Operational Thinking," *Learning and Instruction* 1 (1991): 119–127.

6. J. Piaget, *Biologie et Connaissance* (Paris: Gallimard, 1967).

7. M. Glachan and P. Light, "Peer Interaction and Learning: Can Two Wrongs Make a Right?" in *Social Cognition,* ed. G. Butterworth and P. Light (Brighton, U.K.: Harvester, 1982).

8. W. Doise, *Groups and Individuals* (Cambridge: Cambridge University Press, 1978).

9. L. Vygotsky, *Mind in Society: The Development of Higher Psychological Processes* (Cambridge, Mass.: Harvard University Press, 1978).

10. J. Wertsch, "From Social Interaction to Higher Psychological Processes: A Clarification and Application of Vygotsky's Theory," *Human Development* 22 (1979): 1–22.

11. D. Wood, J. Bruner, and G. Ross, "The Role of Tutoring in Problem-Solving," *Journal of Child Psychology and Psychiatry* 17 (1976): 89–100.

12. S. McNaughton and J. Leyland, "The Shift in Focus of Maternal Tutoring across Different Difficulty Levels on a Problem-Solving Task," *British Journal of Developmental Psychology* 8 (1990): 147–155.

13. Ibid.; D. Wood, H. Wood, and D. Middleton, "An Experimental Evaluation of Four Face-to-Face Teaching Strategies," *International Journal of Behavioural Development* 1 (1978): 131–147; M. Pratt, P. Kerig, P. Cowan, and C. Pape Cowan, "Mothers and Fathers Teaching Three Year Olds: Authoritative Parenting and Adult Scaffolding of Young Children's Learning," *Developmental Psychology* 24 (1988): 832–839.

14. Vygotsky, *Mind in Society.*

15. Pratt et al., "Mothers and Fathers Teaching Three Year Olds."

16. Wood et al., "An Experimental Evaluation of Four Face-to-Face Teaching Strategies."

17. Ibid., p. 79.

18. Ibid.

19. Ibid.

20. B. Radziszewska and B. Rogoff, "Guided Participation in Planning Imaginary Errands with Skilled Adult or Peer Partners," *Developmental Psychology* 27 (1991): 381–389.

21. Ibid.
22. J. Bruner and H. Kenney, "Representation and Mathematical Learning," *Monograph of the Society for Research in Child Development* 30(1) (1965): 50–59.
23. M. Donaldson, *Children's Minds* (Glasgow: Collins/Fontana, 1978).
24. M. Gauvain and B. Rogoff, "Influence of the Goal on Children's Exploration and Memory of Large Scale Space," *Developmental Psychology* 22 (1986): 72–77.
25. J. Glick, "Cognitive Development in Cultural Perspective," in *Review of Child Development Research*, vol. 4, ed. F. Horowitz et al. (Chicago: University of Chicago Press, 1975).
26. J. Skeen, B. Rogoff, and S. Ellis, "Categorization by Children and Adults in Communication Contexts," *International Journal of Behavioural Development* 6 (1983): 213–220.
27. Donaldson, *Children's Minds.*
28. Ibid.; M. Cole and S. Scribner, *Culture and Thought: A Psychological Introduction* (New York: Wiley, 1974).
29. R. Hartley, "Imagine You're Clever," *Journal of Child Psychology and Psychiatry and Allied Disciplines*, 27 (1986): 383–398.
30. M. Seligman, *Helplessness: On Depression, Development and Death* (San Francisco: Freeman, 1975).
31. M. Scheirer and R. Kraut, "Increasing Educational Achievement Via Self-Concept Change," *Review of Educational Research* 49 (1979): 131–150.
32. Ibid.
33. E. Moore, "Family Socialization and the IQ Test Performance of Traditionally and Transracially Adopted Black Children," *Developmental Psychology* 22 (1986): 317–326.
34. R. M. Gagne, "Contributions of Learning to Human Development," *Psychological Review* 75 (1968): 177–191; J. Piaget, *Genetic Epistemology* (New York: Columbia University Press, 1968).
35. B. Rogoff, *Apprenticeship in Thinking: Cognitive Development in Social Context* (New York: Oxford University Press, 1990); B. Rogoff, M. Gauvain, and S. Ellis, "Development Viewed in Its Cultural Context," in *Developmental Psychology: An*

Advanced Textbook, ed. M. Barrister and M. Lamb, pp. 533–571 (Hillsdale, N.J.: Erlbaum, 1984).

36. Ibid.
37. Ibid.

6 / CONCLUSIONS

1. J. Piaget, *Genetic Epistemology* (New York: Columbia University Press, 1968).
2. J. Fodor, *The Modularity of Mind* (Cambridge, Mass.: MIT Press, 1983); H. Gardner, *Frames of Mind: The Theory of Multiple Intelligences* (London, Paladin Books, 1985).
3. A. Karmiloff-Smith, *Beyond Modularity* (Cambridge, Mass.: Bradford Books, MIT Press, 1992).
4. Piaget, *Genetic Epistemology.*
5. R. Siegler, "Three Aspects of Cognitive Development," *Cognitive Psychology* 8 (1976): 481–520.

Suggested Reading

G. Butterworth and P. Light, eds., *Social Cognition* (Brighton, U.K.: Harvester, 1982).

S. Carey, *Conceptual Change in Childhood* (Cambridge, Mass., and London: MIT Press, 1985).

M. Donaldson, *Children's Minds* (Glasgow: Collins/Fontana, 1978).

J. Piaget, *Genetic Epistemology* (New York: Columbia University Press, 1968).

B. Rogoff, M. Gauvain, and S. Ellis, "Development Viewed in Its Cultural Context," in *Developmental Psychology: An Advanced Textbook*, ed. M. Barrister and M. Lamb, pp. 533–571 (Hillsdale, N.J.: Erlbaum, 1984).

R. Siegler, ed., *Children's Thinking: What Develops?* (Hillsdale, N.J.: Erlbaum, 1978).

R. Siegler and E. Jenkins, *How Children Discover New Strategies* (Hillsdale, N.J.: Erlbaum, 1989).

A. Slater and J. Bremner, eds., *Infant Development* (London: Erlbaum, 1989).

Credits

Figure 5: From P. Wason and P. Johnson-Laird, *The Psychology of Reasoning* (London: Batsford, 1972). Reprinted by permission of B. T. Batsford, Ltd.

Figure 6: From P. Kellman and E. Spelke, "Perception of Partly Occluded Objects in Infancy," *Cognitive Psychology* 15 (1983): 483–524. Reprinted by permission of Academic Press.

Figure 8: From R. Siegler, "Three Aspects of Cognitive Development," *Cognitive Psychology* 8 (1976): 481–520. Reprinted by permission of Academic Press.

Figure 9: From M. Chi, P. J. Feltovich, and R. Glaser, "Categorisation and Representation of Physics Problems by Experts and Novices," *Cognitive Science* 5 (1981): 121–152. Reprinted by permission of Ablex Publishing Corporation.

Figure 10: From W. Fabricius, "The Development of Forward Search in Preschoolers," *Child Development* 59 (1988): 1473–1488. Reprinted by permission of the Society for Research in Child Development.

Figure 11: From D. Klahr and M. Robinson, "Formal Assessment of Problem-Solving and Planning Processes in Preschool Children," *Cognitive Psychology* 13 (1981): 113–148. Reprinted by permission of Academic Press.

Figure 12: From A. Karmiloff-Smith, "Micro- and Macro-developmental Changes in Language Acquisition and Other Representational Systems," *Cognitive Science* 3 (1979): 81–118. Reprinted by permission of Ablex Publishing Corporation.

Figure 13: From A. Karmiloff-Smith, *Beyond Modularity: A De-*

velopmental Perspective on Cognitive Science (Cambridge: Bradford Books, MIT Press, 1992). Reprinted by permission of MIT Press.

Figures 15, 16, 17, 18, 21: From R. Wales and S. Thornton, "Psychological Issues in Modelling Creativity," in *Artificial Intelligence and Creativity*, ed. T. Dartnall (Dordrecht, The Netherlands: Kluwer, 1994). Reprinted by permission of Kluwer Academic Publishers.

Figure 24: From D. Wood, *How Children Think and Learn* (Oxford: Blackwell, 1988). Reprinted by permission of Basil Blackwell, Ltd.

Figure 25: From B. Radziszewska and B. Rogoff, "Children's Guided Participation in Planning Imaginary Errands with Skilled Adult or Peer Partners," *Developmental Psychology* 27 (1991): 381–389. Reprinted by permission of the American Psychological Association.

Figure 26: From M. Gauvain and B. Rogoff, "Influences of the Goal on Children's Exploration and Memory of Large-Scale Space," *Developmental Psychology* 22 (1986): 72–77. Reprinted by permission of the American Psychological Association.

Index